DANCING WITH RICHES

IN STEP WITH THE ENERGY OF CHANGE
USING ACCESS CONSCIOUSNESS® TOOLS

DANCING

WITH RICHES

WITH EMPOWERMENT
COACH AND CERTIFIED
FACILITATOR WORLDWIDE
KASS THOMAS

REDFeather™
MIND | BODY | SPIRIT

4880 Lower Valley Road, Atglen, PA 19310

OTHER SCHIFFER BOOKS ON RELATED SUBJECTS:

As You Feel, So You Heal: A Write of Passage,
Donna DeNomme, ISBN 978-0-7643-5810-4

Get Positive Live Positive: Clearing the Negativity from Your Life,
Melinda D. Carver, ISBN 978-0-7643-5291-1

Cover design by Molly Shields
Type set in Blanch/Montserrat
ISBN: 978-0-7643-6154-8
Printed in India

Published by Red Feather Mind, Body, Spirit
An imprint of Schiffer Publishing, Ltd.
4880 Lower Valley Road
Atglen, PA 19310
Phone: (610) 593-1777; Fax: (610) 593-2002
E-mail: Info@schifferbooks.com
Web: www.redfeathermbs.com

For our complete selection of fine books on this and related subjects, please visit our website at www.schifferbooks.com. You may also write for a free catalog.

Schiffer Publishing's titles are available at special discounts for bulk purchases for sales promotions or premiums. Special editions, including personalized covers, corporate imprints, and excerpts, can be created in large quantities for special needs. For more information, contact the publisher.

We are always looking for people to write books on new and related subjects. If you have an idea for a book, please contact us at proposals@schifferbooks.com.

CONTENTS

ABOUT THE BOOK

"What can I add to my life today that will bring me more ease, more joy, and more of an exuberant expression of living?" is a question I have lived by all my life. Though the world of metaphysics fascinated me all along, in my initial years I wasn't aware that I was living by this question. Much later, as my desire to live more consciously continued to expand, my journey of self-discovery and empowerment brought me to some courses of Access Consciousness®, founded by Gary Douglas. This opened up a whole new world for me. It provided me with tools that allowed me to acknowledge what I have always known to be true: a life filled with love, laughter, and abundance is available to all of us. We just have to choose it.

It was my sheer desire and demand for my life to continue opening up to new and greater possibilities that had always kept me going. Even when no one around me could see it or believe it, I never stopped seeking, I never stopped asking, and I never stopped inviting more into my life. Access Consciousness and the people who use the tools of Access are a confirmation that I am not alone in this pursuit.

This book is about my life and how I have lived it, and how I use the tools of Access Consciousness to expand it even more. It is about how I have transformed negative into positive and come through a winner even in limiting situations. It is about how I have taken risks to avoid predictable and undesirable futures. It is about how I have continually evolved, followed the flow of energy (my intuition, my instinct), and created movement even when the waters around me were stagnant. I have successfully come through many situations that I have seen cripple others or stop them in their tracks. I am grateful for my strength of character, my resolve, my willpower, and my constitution. I am also grateful to have encountered Access at the very moment in my life when most people begin to settle for what they already have, instead of continuing to strive for more.

I hope this book invites you to see all that is possible for you, no matter how many times you think you have succeeded or failed. No matter what your dreams or fears are. No matter how perfect or disastrous you think or thought your life to be. Believe me, something greater is always possible. The mantra of Access is "All of life comes to me with Ease and Joy and Glory®." Who would not want more of that? This book is for anyone who is willing to look inward. Be in the moment. Go with the flow and redirect that flow whenever needed. And marvel as the magic unfolds.

Though the tools in this book have been allocated to specific chapters (for easy reading and comprehension), they are interchangeable. Any tool can be used in any situation. Once you get in the groove, you'll know how to allow your intuition and energy to take the lead.

There is no right or wrong method or technique. No knowledge that you have to additionally acquire. The beauty of this path is that no one and nothing is more vital and valuable than you. Especially when it comes to planning and creating your future. You are the creator of your life, your reality, and it is your point of view (POV) that creates your reality. If you are willing to change your POV, you can create the life you desire.

This is a how-to book. It shows you how to incorporate these tools into your daily life and alter your way of thinking. It aids you in adapting to change effortlessly so you can create more. You may be able to save a lot of time, effort, and heartache by reading this book and utilizing these verbal processes. Are you interested in creating a reality that works for you and goes far beyond your imagination?

After over a decade of conducting workshops and conferences, meeting thousands of participants across the globe, I got privy to another subtle reality—YOU are the best version of you that exists on the planet. *No one else does you better than you.* When you are willing to connect with the energy of you, you can easily recognize what is a contribution to your vibration and what is not. Only then can you truly begin dancing with the riches of *your* life.

How does it get any better than that?

ABOUT THE AUTHOR

KASS THOMAS

*If you are on a journey and you are not pleased
with the direction it is taking, maybe it is time
to change tracks!*

Kass's life has been nothing short of an adventure. Having started working at the early age of twelve, she has had a sense of pride, commitment, and passion for everything she has ever done: from managing off-Broadway theatre productions at the start of her career in New York; to working in the hospitality industry at five-star hotels (where she won concierge of the year from *Where Magazine*, New York edition); to starting her own film production company with a friend in Italy; to organizing and working in the film and television industry, at international festivals, and in sales and distribution; to finally finding her true calling as an empowerment and life coach, helping people all over the world optimize their potential and see the brilliance of who they really are.

Kass is also an international bestselling author, trainer, and certified facilitator of Access Consciousness®. She conducts private sessions, group training, and workshops on a variety of topics, using her expertise in communication and many of the pragmatic tools of Access Consciousness.

Kass continues to change tracks even today, and with each new experience she expands who she is and what she loves doing.

Born in Boston, Massachusetts, Kass comes from an unconventional family. Both her parents left their previous partners to be together and raise Kass. Her family environment included people from various ethnicities and backgrounds, which instilled a multicultural and global curiosity in her. She obtained an undergraduate degree in journalism and mass communication and then went on to postgraduate studies in theatrical management, both at New York University. Ultimately, she traveled to diverse locations, such as France, Spain, and Italy, mastering those languages in order to be able to communicate more directly with the local people there. Her love of travel, diversity, and inclusion of different cultures still prevails today.

In addition to being a certified Access facilitator, she is also one of the few Access three-day body class facilitators in the world. Her journey with Access Consciousness started in 2003. In 2006, she got her certified facilitator's license and in 2007 invited the founder, Gary Douglas, and cocreator, Dr. Dain Heer, to hold their first European classes in Italy. She was instrumental in the development of the Access language and translation programs for many years, helping extend it from four to 176 countries and over thirty languages.

Her workshops reach a variety of people and places, including Australia, Austria, Bahrain, Brazil, Canada, China, Croatia, the Czech Republic, Estonia, France, Germany, Holland, Hungary, India, Indonesia, Israel, Italy, Japan, Kuwait, Morocco, the Netherlands, New Zealand, Poland, Russia, Saudi Arabia, Slovenia, South Africa, Spain, Switzerland, Turkey, the UAE, the UK, the United States, and more.

In her journey, she has encountered and facilitated over 1,000 workshops and assisted over 10,000 people, including Ray Charles, Madonna, Denzel

Washington, Whoopi Goldberg, Michelle Pfeiffer, Miles Davis, Morgan Freeman, and others.

As a result of her many adventures, she authored the bestselling book *7steps to Flawless Communication*, which is available in over fifteen languages, including Czech, Chinese, Japanese, Polish, Turkish, and many others. Her second book, *Dancing with Riches*, launched first in French in the spring of 2019, will also be available in multiple languages.

When she is not traveling the world, facilitating classes and workshops, Kass is home in Italy with her husband, Marco, enjoying some of their many shared interests, including tennis, dancing, jazz, singing (and she knows all the words to every song!), and good food. In fact, you can often find pictures on Instagram of the amazing international dinners at her home, prepared by her husband for friends and family. Their boutique bed & breakfast, Villino Corbelli, situated in their 1920s villa in Rome, has received top reviews for almost twenty years.

It fills me with joy to watch how quickly and easily someone can start creating more in their life, with their body and their financial situation, just by choosing to do so.

SOME OF HER FREQUENTLY USED INSPIRATIONAL QUESTIONS INCLUDE

What is it that fills you with joy?

What is your unique brand of magic?

What gifts and talents do you have that come so easily to you that you don't even consider them valuable?

What can I add to my life today that would create more joy and money right away?

For more information on where Kass is and what she is doing today, see below.

Find Kass on social media:

KASS THOMAS WEBSITE: www.kassthomas.com

ACCESS CONSCIOUSNESS WEBSITE: www.accessconsciousness.com/kassthomas

3 STEPS: www.3STEPS.us

7STEPS: www.7steps.us

FACEBOOK: The Art of Being Kass

INSTAGRAM: The Art of Being Kass

LINKEDIN: Kass Thomas

YOUTUBE: Being Kass

ACHNOWLEDGMENTS

I am eternally grateful for all that life has offered me, and for the way the Universe has always had my back. I have experienced some very "interesting" situations in my life. No matter how rough the waters have been, I have remained undeterred and have sailed forward because the Universe has always guided me. It has invited me to continually explore my true nature and create more. And I am not done yet.

I would like to thank the founder of Access Consciousness, Gary Douglas, and its cocreator Dr. Dain Heer, for the remarkable work they do, and for the amazing beings they are. It is not easy being catalysts of change, and it is certainly a choice that continues to create so much more in the lives of millions of people. I am so grateful for their dedication and for the contribution they have been to my life.

I am grateful to all those people who have interacted with me and used the tools of Access Consciousness and the *7 steps to Flawless Communication*.

I have a phenomenal family and group of friends who have been extremely supportive of me and all that I believe in. To begin with, I am happy I chose to come to the family I did. Jean and Cliff, my mom and dad, always loved me unconditionally, as did my godfathers, Jimmy Jones and Tommy; my father-in-law, Luciano; my brother Gregg; and my former boss Carlo Bixio. Even after they moved on, they still watch over me. Thank you.

Gratitude to my sister, Jett (born Kim), a brilliant artist who cared for our folks up to their last breaths, my brother Cliff, and my godmother, Mummy Gail, who has always loved "her little poopsie." Thank you.

I thank my husband, Marco Corbelli. It is my absolute joy to have chosen to be in a relationship so nurturing and supportive and that has provided me with the space to be who I truly am. His mom and family too have always been a great support to me, and for that I say: "Grazie mille, davvero!"

I have immense gratitude for my longtime friends Andrea, Leslie, Ari, Karen, Wicki, Annabelle, Carmen, Nilda, Isabel, Hamida, Delphine, Nnenna, and many others. Their unconditional love and support have helped me sail through some of the most intense episodes of my life. If I have forgotten to mention your name, please remind me, and I'll make sure to mention you in my next book.

I thank Boston, New York, Paris, Rome, and all the other cities I have and will visit, for being such a huge contribution in my life. I love the land, the languages, the cultures, the people, and the experiences that have helped me grow exponentially.

I thank Trédaniel and Schiffer Publishing, Ilham, Tea, Marina, Alessandro, Petra, Cathy Maillard, Todd Schuster, Chris, McClure, Peggy Kellar, Amy Fisher, and Pete Schiffer for opening up their doors and contributing in tangible and intangible ways to make this book a reality.

Writing this book has been an amazing journey. It is full of incidents that have shaped my approach to life and my personality. Going back in the past, reliving those awarenesses, and penning them in this book . . . what an illuminating process it has been! I am grateful to Ritu Ferrao for her patience in helping me bring this book to life. I couldn't have done it without her. Her dedication to excellence has inspired me to write more. After hours of conversations, rereads and rewrites, culling out instances that seemed most contributive, threading this book together into a smooth narrative, has been quite an enriching experience for both of us.

Last, I want to thank Myself. Me, Myself, and I, and my Body—my lifetime companion. "We've come a long way, baby." This body has stuck with me and allowed me to do a lot, without ever giving up or quitting on me. Thanks to it, I've had unbelievable stamina and infinite energy to achieve a lot more in life than I could have possibly imagined. For all this and some more, I am extremely grateful. Now as I embark on my next adventures, there is one question that continually shows up: What else is possible, now?

WHAT IS ACCESS CONSCIOUSNESS?

Only by expanding our consciousness beyond the problem can we transform a situation into a possibility and create a different outcome.

Access Consciousness is a set of life-transformational tools that empower us to know that we know. This allows us to attain a level of clarity so we can sieve out the judgments that limit us, and create a life from a space of infinite possibilities.

Founded by Gary Douglas in 1995 and cocreated by Dr. Dain Heer in 2000, Access Consciousness is prevalent in over 170 countries today. This worldwide phenomenon radically changed my life at multiple levels and in more ways than I could ever have imagined.

Unlike many other modalities that clear limitations associated with words, Access Consciousness clears the energy around them, erasing their dense effects across Time and Space. How does it get any better than that?

Apart from this, its beauty lies in its simplicity and the speed with which change occurs. Any individual from any walk of life can change their existing reality by merely changing their points of view and exercising these easy and simple tools in their daily life, just the way I did.

No problem can be solved from the same level of consciousness that created it.

—Albert Einstein (noted physicist)

THE CLEARING STATEMENT

Since I have used this statement throughout the book, it is essential I explain in detail what the statement means. We don't necessarily need to understand the Clearing Statement for it to show miraculous results in our lives. As a matter of fact, it is meant to go around our thinking mind and reach that part of our brain where all our answers and truths are easily accessible. But since our need for logic and tangibility seldom eludes us, I will quench that thirst.

One of the most profound and potent tools of Access Consciousness is its Clearing Statement: *Right and Wrong, Good and Bad, POD and POC, All 9, Shorts, Boys, and Beyonds®*. Let's say it is an energetic broom that clears away any dust that blocks or limits our points of view, and thus our lives.

Whenever we ask a question about a particular situation, it brings up all the energies we have around it—all judgments, definitions, thoughts, feelings, and emotions—that don't allow us to see the situation clearly. It is like trying to resolve the problem from within it. When we ask a question about it and apply the Clearing Statement to these energies that come up, it creates more space between us and the situation or problem. This space allows us to see different possibilities. Then, we can make a choice based on new and fresh information.

So, what the Clearing Statement really does is to dissolve the density and fog. It gives us more clarity and helps us create our lives through a series of choices instead of living through reactions and resistance.

It works wonders.

Note to self: *Please know that you can NOT destroy and uncreate what is true for you. What goes away is anything and everything that limits you from being all of you.* So, attach the Clearing Statement to any question, and you will release any stuck energies in no time.

Here is how it works: We ask a question about a situation or dilemma, and then we ask to destroy and uncreate all the energies that come up about the situation: *Everything that is (all those energies known and unknown), let's destroy and uncreate it all now, please? Times a godzillion, Right and Wrong, Good and Bad, POD and POC, All 9, Shorts, Boys, and Beyonds.*

Destroy and uncreate it: Uncreate is a made-up term. It basically means let's stop feeding our creative juices to something that isn't working for us.

Times a godzillion: It is an incalculable number. It is so huge that only God knows how big it is. So we are asking the effects of the Clearing Statement to go beyond our calculations.

Right and Wrong, Good and Bad: These stand for all our judgments.

POC: Point of creation (wherever the limitation started in the first place)

POD: Point of destruction (wherever that limitation started destroying our possibility to choose something different, irrespective of Time and Space)

POD and POC is a way of breaking that cycle that keeps us operating under the glass ceiling of limited possibilities.

All 9: The number 9 stands for the nine layers of stuff we clear with this Clearing Statement.

Shorts: What's meaningful and meaningless about this; the punishments and rewards for it.

Boys: These are areas where we have worked hard on something for a long time yet haven't gotten the desired effect. Sometimes there is more than one source causing the issue. Boys takes care of all the origins of the stated situation.

Beyonds: This too, like "uncreate," is a made-up word. It doesn't mean "beyond the stars." They are feelings or sensations we get in our bodies that cause hindrance. They stop us dead in our tracks.

You don't have to remember the entire Clearing Statement. You can simply say, "POC & POD all that," and it still does the trick. In fact, that is the beauty of Access. It is not based on logic; it is about the energy. Now that you know what the Clearing Statement is about, now that you have gotten the energy of it, you can just say, "POC & POD all that," and it will work. How does it get any better than that?

For more information, you can visit www.theclearingstatement.com.

CHAPTER 1:

DECODING THE REAL YOU: FROM ONE TO ONENESS

It had been a while since I had connected with the expansiveness of nature. I had been feeling a bit contracted for a few days, so I wanted to step out and commune with Mother Earth, get entrenched in the potent simplicity of the planet. I remembered one of my friends had suggested that I attend to my pale-looking garden, sooner rather than later. In my absence the plants were looking a bit lifeless. They needed my energy. I figured this would be a perfect exercise to reconnect with Mother Earth and help rejuvenate my garden at the same time.

As I woke up, before I got consumed by work—reading text messages, getting down to responding to emails, and the like—I decided to step outside and savor my little spot of heaven. My garden. Oh dear! How could "heaven" look this sad? No worries; I'll talk to my little green patch and pump up the energy. I knew I would be able to add some vibrancy back into the flora. After all, that was my specialty. I was good at animating anyone and anything. It was my job. I was confident the status quo would change. Thus began my being-one-with-nature exercise.

"Hi there, flower, how are you?" No response. I didn't feel a thing. I waited a bit and asked again, "How's it going?" I waited a bit longer. Still nothing. No response. Normally if you call out to something three times consecutively, it allows you to connect. I repeated myself. Nah, nothing. I walked a little deeper into the garden, placing my bare feet on the ground, and my hand on the trunk of my favorite tree. "Hey, tree, long time no see. How are you doing? Do you need a bit of my energy? I'm trying to connect with you." Alas, my magic wasn't working. I had done this drill in the past. It had always been a blissful experience, but today nothing was happening. What the heck was going on? What was wrong?

As my struggle to interact with nature continued, I took a couple of steps farther and reached my fence. On the other side stood two gorgeous-looking dogs. They had been around for long over a decade. If flora didn't work, maybe fauna would. I was excited. Well, work it did. They looked me up and down and made an instant connection with me, as if to say, "Really? We mean, really? Honey, you're the one who needs the communication and contribution here. Are YOU willing to receive it?"

Wow! My whole world melted instantly. My body relaxed, and the peace I had been trying so hard to give to nature was delivered to me with a simple gaze from the doggies. I was attempting to give something I didn't have. What I really needed to do was relax and receive. That revelation hit me like a bolt of lightning, illuminating, sharp, and potent. I had gotten into the "doing" to relax myself (the exercise of connecting with nature)—rather than being relaxed and allowing myself to receive from nature.

BEING VS. DOING

Consciously or otherwise, we usually have set points of view about how we should behave in a particular setting. For example, earlier when I would be out in nature, I would coax myself to feel one with it. On a beach, if I found myself reading messages on my phone or responding to emails, I would get upset and force myself into relaxing. Why was I on the phone when I could be enjoying the sweetness of doing nothing? Like they say, "Il dolce far niente" in Italian. "Relax," I would tell myself. "Receive the energy of the sea." It was all about how it should look. But "shoulds" seldom contribute to build something greater. They aren't creative and are nongenerative. "Shoulds" bring along with them only an avalanche of self-judgment.

Doing is the activity of the mind, while *Being* is a natural extension of who we are. We can pretend to be connected, to be present in the moment, but when we truly are, our mind and body are in communion. We feel one with the universe. It is in this space that we are really connected with our core being. Many times, it is a completely different experience from what we may have anticipated it to be.

The sporadic appearance of this exhilarating phenomenon of truly being connected with the universe may be demotivating at times, but its frequency can be increased with regular practice and determination. Many times, people don't even recognize that they are not connected because they have never beeh. Everything changes once they experience the ecstasy of this communion.

Whether or not you have ever felt this union, keep reading because you'll know what I am talking about. Before, if you were unaware of this possibility it was just the way you were, so it wasn't demotivating. It was just the way you were. Once you know this possibility exists, either you can choose to be demotivated by how rarely it shows up, or you can be exhilarated knowing you have access to it. I would rather choose to be inspired by the fact that I have a possibility in hand. What about you?

If you feel tension in your body, or, say, you are rigid about your way of being, chances are that you are going into the "shoulds" of things—"What should I do?" "How should I carry myself?" "Where should I go?" "How should I get there?" The moment you establish true connection with YOU, a space opens up. You recognize the possibility of living life without any mind chatter. You become aware of the fact that the rigidity and barriers you had put up were really just your modus operandi. Now you know something else exists.

To move forward, all you have to do is recognize and acknowledge the times when these moments of union show up. Understand that these are actually points of departure from your old way of being, and not objects of self-judgment.

Everywhere you see a possibility—but are demotivated by the fact that you are not choosing them—will you recognize what a gift it is to acknowledge the possibility? By recognizing that gift, you are already choosing a proactive approach instead of a demotivating attitude. All the self-deprecating judgments that aren't allowing you to contribute to your growth, times a godzillion, will you destroy and uncreate it all now, please? Right and Wrong, Good and Bad, POD and POC, All 9, Shorts, Boys, and Beyonds.

At such moments, you usually have three doors available to you:

Door 1: *The demotivating option*—you open the door (or Pandora's box) to examine every single time you haven't done what you could be doing, concentrating on all the places and the number of times such things have happened in your life. It leads you into a vicious downward spiral of negativity and looking backward, not forward.

Door 2: *Pretend it never happened*—you open the door to oblivion, business as usual; it couldn't happen again because, in fact, nothing happened—it was just a moment. You feel the moment(s) of communion with your Being, but you continue leading your life believing the dictate of your mind (rather than listening to your intuition). Like always, you keep feeding your Ego over choosing a path that truly contributes to your overall growth.

Door 3: *Acknowledge and accept this occurrence*—you open up **Door 3** to see what else is possible; what else can you explore here? You discover that one million other doors lie beyond that one door. No tunnels, no brick walls, not oblivion—only infinite possibilities, choices, and contributions. "Wow! What would it take to have more of that? How cool is it that I have this option?!" This leads you to a space of infinite possibilities—different choices you get to pick from.

I took my time with imbibing this way of being. Sure, there were moments when I would find myself entering **Door 1**, but with regular practice, I progressed to getting more nonjudgmental. There is always a learning curve that has to do with anything new we do. There may be an initial struggle, but with time and practice, it gets easier. Self-doubt gets replaced with expansion and confidence. For example, when learning to ride a bike, we are scared about the initial instability and excited about the possibility of getting over it. We wobble. We fall. With practice we gain more assuredness, and one day we'll simply hop on the bike and enjoy the ride.

DECODING THE REAL YOU

To be integrated with our core being, we first have to know who we truly are, don't we? An ample number of times, we become someone or do something that isn't in sync with our true nature. This usually occurs when we are trying to fit in or make peace with a person or situation.

For instance, both my mom and dad were in their respective relationships when they first met. It was love at first sight. Something clicked and they could not deny it. Lord knows they tried. In fact, they didn't officially get together until ten years later. The family had gotten my mother married to a good-looking, well-liked guy. She had a two-year-old daughter (my half sister) from her first marriage. They seemed to be the "perfect couple." Yet, when she met my dad, she decided to part ways with her first husband, Louis Thomas, because she had never experienced this frenzy of ecstasy before.

How many times have you let your heart guide your life? Making a choice for yourself does not necessarily mean choosing against other people. Do you make a choice for you, or have you always obeyed the norm laid down by society and your family, and killed the real you? Each time you have chosen to be someone you are not, only so you could fit in and not ruffle feathers, times a godzillion, will you destroy and uncreate it all now, please? Right and Wrong, Good and Bad, POD and POC, All 9, Shorts, Boys, and Beyonds.

My dad, on the other hand, had been a Casanova all his life. He was no longer married to his first wife when he met my mom, but he was living with a woman. He also had a few flings on the side. Having fathered two sons at a very young age (with his first wife), he left her and his sons behind when she started doing drugs and dating other men. Eventually, his first wife died of a drug overdose. Many years later, when his sons were in their teens, they resurfaced in his life. I was thirteen when I first met my two half brothers.

There were moments in my life when I would ask Mom to divorce Dad. He was mean, rude, and unkind, even. A complete misfit in the social circle, my parents were hardly ever invited to social events. It took me many years to realize how much my mom truly loved my dad. Sometimes, though, I wonder—had she never regretted her decision of going against everyone in the family and marrying a man who was so tough to live with? Who was the real she?

Sometimes in order to make a choice that goes against the norm, you feel you have to be rebellious and then keep defending all the consequences or actions. Have you ever been in such a kind of dilemma? Did you ever take a stand and live by your decision at the cost of your self-esteem and identity? Did you regret it later?

OUR POINT OF VIEW = OUR REALITY

I was already six when my parents finally sorted out their past and decided to tie the knot. Since my mom was still legally married to her first husband, "Tommy," my sister's father, when I was born, I got his surname—Thomas. Once my parents were officially a couple, we four—Mom, Dad, my sister, and I—began living together as a family.

It wasn't always easy for us—the new family—to live happily together. Even though my dad and sister were living in the same house, for years they did not speak to one another. Yet, it was never about my parents and me operating as one unit, and my sister the other. I had always worked hard to ensure she never felt left out. I perennially tried to make peace, playing the role of intermediary—trying hard to be so much the energy of no separation, no judgment, and no exclusion.

Even though they were excluding one another from their lives, I did my best not to let that happen. This balancing act continued right up to when my dad was dying, losing his senses and his mind. He was keen on maintaining the separation with my sister, even trying to exclude her from his will, but I wasn't comfortable with that option. Yet again, my role of an eternal peacemaker took center stage, and I preferred to have him die without a will, rather than perpetuate the lie of separation. This role cost me innumerable bureaucratic and economic complications after his death.

Have you ever fought someone else's battle so hard that it became yours? Yet, you didn't mind paying a price for it, even if it were a steep one to pay?

WHEN ROLE PLAY BECOMES REAL

In spite of my family being comprised of one half sister and two half brothers, I never saw any separation. The only aspect I recognized later was that I had overcompensated for what I had perceived as lack in their lives. I believed that not having a loving father, or having no mother, was a disadvantage. I presumed it was my duty and responsibility to be more inclusive. I also felt I had no right to complain about anything. After all, I had both parents. I had a perfect life, a presumed privilege I never took advantage of. I only allowed it to take advantage of me.

"What if I never had to assume this role? What if I never felt responsible for other people's choices? What would my life have been like?" I ponder over these permutations sometimes.

All of this diplomacy of constantly ensuring no one is offended or hurt led me to a maze of situations where I found myself never being disliked by anyone. All at the cost of having an identity crisis. When certain individuals didn't take to me that well, it would perturb me.

Decades later, it dawned on me that people liking or disliking me was completely their choice. It necessarily didn't mean that I had or had not done something. This huge revelation was thanks to Access Consciousness, a radical concept for me at that time, and a catalyst in my drastic transformation.

I realized that the more I was willing to be comfortable in my own skin, the more ease there would be in my life. The constant mind chatter of trying to decipher what others were thinking about me had taken a back seat. No more was I buckling under pressure of trying to make people happy or maintain a certain image I wanted people to have of me. Not that I had ever let it slow me down, but that continuous state of thinking, evaluating, calculating, calibrating, and recalibrating had been exhausting. I hadn't realized how grueling it was until I stopped going through all those experiences. Once I accepted the new way of life, it worked wonders. The ease and comfort of being who I truly was, as opposed to putting in a lot of effort to be inclusive, was a liberating way of life. Funny, now it comes naturally to me. With ease.

How many times have you chosen what is truly best for you? That doesn't mean you have to choose against other people. It only signifies that you are being true to you. Have you ever allowed yourself to be true to your being even if your choice is difficult for others? Everywhere that you choose to be what others expect of you rather than what makes you happy and joyful, times a godzillion, will you destroy and uncreate it all now, please? Right and Wrong, Good and Bad, POD and POC, All 9, Shorts, Boys, and Beyonds.

Now that I have abandoned the tightrope-walking task of pleasing people, I always find myself expanding, reaching for new horizons, new aspirations, new paths to explore. And you know what? People always say how generous and inclusive I am in everything I do. Funny, huh? How does it get better than that?

When you choose what works best for you, which has nothing to do with opposing anyone or defending your actions because it may be difficult for others, people get the energy of it. They get that it isn't about them at all. It simply is about "This is what works for me."

LOST IN THE WEB OF ORIGINALITY AND UNAUTHENTICITY

One of the most powerful questions often used in Access Consciousness is "Who am I being?" When you ask this question, it helps you detect and diagnose the personality traits that you picked up from others, believing they were your own.

Once you establish an authentic connection with yourself, it becomes obvious when you deviate from that link. The question of Who am I being? immediately snaps you out of that autopilot mode of catering to others first and brings you back to being true to yourself—the infinite *Being*.

There was a point in time in my life when I realized I had taken a few qualities of my dad and made them my own. My dad was a complete no-nonsense kind of guy. He was very different from anyone I had ever known. Most others were content with superficial chatter and putting on airs, but not my dad. You had to be real and authentic if you wanted to engage him in conversation. You'd better "shoot straight" (as he would say). He could spot bullshit or a liar from a mile away. His acute sense of awareness helped him gauge people better.

Like my dad, I too couldn't take people telling me things they didn't mean. I would get distracted or irritated, not understanding why I was feeling heavy. It wasn't until I did Access Consciousness that I could articulate what I was really feeling. Lies always made me feel uncomfortable. All the irritation, distraction, and boredom I would feel around liars, I had attributed to low blood sugar or being tired. In actuality, I was picking up on someone trying to hide something or selling me a lie (as if it were the truth). I would exhaust myself trying to make sense out of their invented stories and excuses. Now it just makes me smile. (Ironically, my second husband, Marco, and his mother, Anna, have a similar barometer for bullshit. Hmmm. Interesting.)

WHAT IF . . .

As much as I had admired that quality in my dad, I realized later that he had cut off ties with almost everybody because of his nitpicking nature. My dad had great awareness, but he would often shut the door on people after judging their limiting behavior. If they would have changed later, he wouldn't have ever known because he would never have given them a second chance. Also, just because someone is rigid in one area of their life does not mean that that person has to be that way in other aspects of life too.

How often do we judge people or situations right off the bat and are unable to obtain anything new or different from them? We have already concluded who or what they are. We rarely believe that people or situations can change, or that there may be a possibility of something different showing up. Everywhere that we limit new possibilities by judging them on the basis of the past, times a godzillion, let's destroy and uncreate it all now, please? Right and Wrong, Good and Bad, POD and POC, All 9, Shorts, Boys, and Beyonds.

Now I have a simple philosophy—get the awareness (it is a great quality), but leave the conclusion and judgment behind. It limits what else is possible that might not be obvious in the first encounter. Many times, during the initial meeting, people have their barriers up or are trying too hard to make an impression. They may fumble and falter. That does not necessarily mean that is who they are.

The difference between awareness and judgment is that one leads to more questions and more possibilities, whereas the other shuts the door to everything—good or bad. Be more aware; let go of the limiting judgments.

For example, once a gardener came to my home to clean my gardens. He had been with us for over a decade, so I knew him quite well. After sprucing up a part of the bushes and plants, he decided to step out for lunch. Since the other part of the garden was yet to be done, I called out to him. I even gave him money for gloves and other materials. When he was leaving for lunch, I got this hunch that he wouldn't be coming back that day, but I ignored my hunch and tried to push the situation forward, to go against what I knew, to make it happen anyway. Basically I chose **Door 2**—pretend that what I knew wasn't true didn't exist. I kept waiting for him until late afternoon. In this instance, I had gotten the awareness that he would not come back. Had I just gone with my intuition, I would have saved myself the anger and agony that followed. Also, had I chosen awareness, I wouldn't be self-critical about judging the gardener. I knew he would not come back, because I had witnessed this happen in the past. Yet, I wanted to give him the benefit of doubt. If I was willing not to have a point of view about my observation, I would have known the inevitable (rather than get angry at the situation and myself).

Today, my mindfulness makes me present to the way a particular individual is. Now I'm smart enough to know what that person is capable of doing, what he or she should do, could do, will indeed do, and what he or she will probably never do. This is being aware, not being judgmental. It is a great quality to hone while communicating with people in any situation. And now I'm okay with myself if I am proved wrong. It doesn't rattle me anymore. On the contrary, rather, I am quite willing to be pleasantly surprised.

THE FLIP SIDE OF SYMBIOTIC IDENTITY

Elaborating further on how we unconsciously take on people's personality traits, when we duplicate others' individualities (symbiotic identity), these may not always be pleasant characteristics to possess. There were moments when I would catch myself in the middle of replicating a "dad act." Features that I hadn't liked in him, occasionally I would become them myself. The way I would react in a situation would be eerily similar to how Dad would have behaved in an identical circumstance.

I vividly remember an incident that I had experienced in Paris. As I was looking out the window, I suddenly felt a surge of intense suspicion and negative thoughts consume my mind. I had started complaining and judging a lot. This was an out-of-character behavior for me. I had never had such thoughts. Who did? "Who does this belong to?" I asked (this is a fabulous Access Consciousness question to pop when you have thoughts that make you feel heavy for no apparent reason). I immediately thought of my dad. "Dad, is this you?" I probed. I realized it was him when I felt a sense of relief immediately after asking that question. The judgements and negative thoughts immediately disappeared, and I started seeing the same situation from a space of possibilities. I said, "Thanks, Dad," and laughed in acknowledgment. It was his unique way of communicating to and through me. Energetically, he told me to acknowledge the success I had achieved.

Had I not realized what was happening to me, I would have believed that those thoughts and judgments were mine. I would have started going into the wrongness of me for having them. Instead, here, I was able to be grateful to me and Dad for this amazing revelation. It turned out to be a beautiful day in Paris that opened up lots of new possibilities, including an offer to publish this book!

Every time I think about this incident, it offers me new information. Have you ever felt the same before? Where in your life have you stopped receiving information from past experiences? What if you are willing to look at every present and past moment as new beginnings? What new possibilities for the future would that create? All that prohibits you from revisiting your past, keeping an open mind to receiving additional awareness, times a godzillion, will you destroy and uncreate it all now, please? Right and Wrong, Good and Bad, POD and POC, All 9, Shorts, Boys, and Beyonds.

THE LITMUS TEST

How do we recognize the difference between "Who does this belong to?" and "Who are we truly?"

Ask questions.

Who am I being here? Am I being me or am I being someone else just to fit in this situation? Hang in there for a moment or two, and you will recognize the truth or unauthenticity of you. If you feel happy, relaxed, light, and at ease, the behavior you presented belongs to you. If you feel heavy, stunted, or tight, it is time to bid farewell to that quality or behavior.

The more you are willing to look at something for what it is, the more you are enabled to play with different energies and alter any situation. During these experiences, some uncomfortable energies too may get triggered. Worry not. As you discover things you have been unwilling to look at or have even blocked out, it will help you peel off layers of falsehood—the various selves you have put forward to fit in someone else's reality. You will come closer to recognizing your true self or, more aptly put, the real you.

THE COMPLEXITY OF OUR CONSTRUCTED SELF (THE EGO)

There is never a fixed question or answer that will give you linear and simple solutions to which role you should adorn in any situation. While being subtle and undemanding may work in a certain instance, confronting head-on may be the apt way to take on the world in another situation.

In my first grade, I was a chubby kid who many would bully. I particularly remember two mean girls, Vivian and Freda, who would take advantage of my naivete and make me walk farther away from my house. They would command me to walk up to their block, then point me in the direction to continue in a large circle to get back to my house. I had a feeling that I was walking way out of my way, but if I had questioned or disobeyed them, they would bully me more. I didn't want to ruffle anyone's feathers, so I took the hike.

The scene altered completely when I was in my teens. I was always sincere about my studies, and being a good student was the only way I had known to be. There were a few tall girls who would bump into me or knock down my books in the corridor. Since I was studious and hung out with the nerds, they tried to punish me. They wanted to beat me up at the drop of a hat. Fight back? Who, me? No way. Pretending that I didn't notice their aggression or bombarding them with being extremely kind was more my style. Rise above, go beyond—I believed in this philosophy. But that wasn't working so well. One day, I had had enough. Something snapped within me. I decided I wasn't going to put up with this kind of nonsense for an entire year, or lifetime. I asked for some advice and learned some preliminary boxing moves from my sister's boyfriend, who was a black belt in tae kwon do (a form of martial art).

A few days later, I was at my locker when that group of girls approached to bully me for the umpteenth time. All nervous and jittery, I stood still and took a long, deep breath, repeating in my head what I had learned just days before: keep your fists up to protect your chest and face. If you have to throw a punch, put your shoulder into it and sting like a bee, fast and deadly. I knew this was the moment to stand up for myself. As one of them came forward and grabbed my shoulder to spin me around. I spun around, all right, together with a perfectly placed punch. Everyone—including me—was stunned. This wasn't my personality. My teachers had known me to be friendly and sociable, a good student, not a fighter. What just happened? The group of girls was all looking at me with their mouths open, and they slowly started to back away.

After that incident, no one ever bothered me again. They would clear the path whenever I would come down the hallway with my nerd friends (who were thrilled). I was detained for a week. My mom was very upset for my rowdy behavior, but was I apologetic or ashamed of myself? Hell, no. I knew it was the best choice to make at that time, since it would create so much more ease for my future at the school, and in life. I was feeling so light that I could fly.

Back home, drama of a different kind continued. As my mom stood looking at me with tears in her eyes, trying to figure out "How could this happen to mumma's little girl," my dad also had watery eyes. Just that they were of a different kind. His tears were accompanied with a big, fat grin on his face. The sparkle of pride shined with nothing but admiration for me. He was proud of the way I had stood up for myself. Having spent much of his youth hustling on the streets just to survive, he knew bullies all too well. He knew that this out-of-character move would save me many undesirable situations in the future. Of course, my mom never saw this telepathic exchange. She surely got a whiff of it though. When she turned around to look at him, he quickly hung his head down, as if in shame. He shook his head, using his hand to cover up the ear-to-ear grin.

ALLOWING THE UNIVERSE TO INTERVENE

Being and *Doing* have their rightful places in our lives, but sometimes, Allowance (no fixed point of view) is the key.

Earlier when I would hear people complain about being extremely busy all the time, I would sympathize with them. I realized later that they were the sect of beings who had taken on the onus of performing every task themselves. Delegation wasn't part of their reality. The mountain needs moving? Well, I'd better buckle up and start pushing it. Allowing the universe to smoothen the path wasn't an option.

It is not to say that I hadn't been in their shoes before. I had certainly tried to move a few mountains on my own in the past, but when I got privy to the joy of teamwork, I completely changed my approach to life.

Universe or Mother Nature—or whatever we would like to call this all-encompassing energy—can help us do any task with no resistance, as long as we are willing to divorce ourselves from the belief that we have to be the perpetual doers. Instead of doing a task, what if we could ask it to be a contribution to us? What if we could ask the universe to help us do a task (rather than taking on the responsibility of doing everything ourselves)? Elegance = minimum effort, maximum result. Thank you for this one, Gary.

After an earthquake, we get flooded with support from unexpected sources.

Why? Because then, and sometimes only then, are we willing to receive any and every kind of support. What if we didn't have to wait for distress to knock on our door before we allowed ourselves to enjoy the fruits of seamless manifestation? What would it take not to have to wait to be knocked down before we are willing to receive the contribution of others?

Let me share an example of how the universe always has our back. I was running the house of a very good friend who was ailing. Barring his bedroom, he had rented out all the other rooms. I monitored the upkeep, solved grievances of tenants, and did a few more things for the house while he was in the hospital. It was a stopgap arrangement. Once he would get fit, he would take on the responsibility of running his house again.

He never returned from the hospital; he died after a few months. It is so ironic that it was around the same time when my decade-long marriage had collapsed completely. Had it not been for his empty bedroom, I'd have had no place to go to that night (when I chose to walk away from my first husband). Had this possibility not existed, I might have had to stay in an unlivable situation. Who knows where my life would have led me from there? Who knows where I would be now?

STAY OPEN TO RECEIVING IN VARIED FORMS

There are innumerable ways by which the higher forces reach out to give us a hand, or even walk with us, but we have to be willing to listen and receive it. We have to be willing to receive contribution. Like in the case of accepting aid during an earthquake.

Then again, sometimes, we just have to keep moving forward, be proactive, and keep doing our bit. Who knows what our deeds may lead us to in the future? They may become a blessing without us realizing it then. For example, when I was taking care of my friend's apartment, little had I known then that in the future, that is where I would stay when I left my first marriage behind.

There are various ways by which we can receive abundance from the universe. I can journal an encyclopedia on proof of how I've gotten messages in diverse forms, from different avenues. I'll share another case that highlights this aspect more clearly.

I was driving from Los Angeles to Las Vegas at five o'clock in the morning. There was more traffic than I had anticipated at that time of the morning, and I was in a hurry. I had to get my childhood girlfriend Andrea to the airport in time. She was going back to our hometown, Boston, by the first flight. After many years, we had managed to carve out a small, two-day vacation together. She had booked that flight so we could do both—spend as much time together as we possibly could, and she could be back in time for her work.

We enjoyed the beauty of the sunrise over the desert and sipped hot beverages. That helped us stay awake and alert. We were trying hard not to worry about her missing the flight. To take our mind off the tension, we turned on the radio. At that early hour, all we got were stations that played evangelical content.

I was confident the universe had our back. I just wanted to identify the signal it would send this time to let us know that we had made the right choice, and that everything would be all right. I suggested we ask a question: "Universe, can you show us some magic, please?" Randomly, our search ended at a preacher talking about his unwavering determination to open a new church in London. Everyone had said it was impossible, but he never lost faith, he fought against all odds, and eventually he made it happen. The preacher added, at the very end, "Expect and don't underestimate the supernatural. When you feel a stirring in your heart, know that these are messages from the Lord." Voilà! Using different words, different examples (I have never desired to open up a church; not yet, anyway), but the message was loud and clear. I had felt the stirring in my heart, all right.

The power of determination and never giving in, never giving up and never quitting, even in the face of adversity and disbelievers, makes everything possible. That is when you open up the space for magic, and the manifestation of miracles is possible.

Elated with our self-discovery, Andrea and I digressed to discussing other topics. It is amazing how countless religions have similar teachings based on a singular philosophy; only the names and approaches differ. If you don't allow words to cause hindrance and separation, then Lord, Jesus, God, Allah, Buddha, Ganesh, Messiah, Miracles, Magic, Universe, Love . . . aren't they all referring to one thing? Energy.

As the famous physicist Albert Einstein once quoted: Everything is Energy, and that's all there is to it. Match the frequency of the reality you want, and you cannot help but get that reality. It can be no other way.

As Andrea and I followed the energy of least resistance, going with the flow (to keep ourselves from getting tensed about missing her flight), we made it to the airport in plenty of time. We even got to share another hot cup of coffee, and a really warm hug before her check-in.

ENGAGE ENERGY FOR CLARITY

Apart from allowing the universe to come to our aid, there are other methods to request and receive contributions. Every animate and inanimate thing has a specific vibration in and around it. It is an energy. We can communicate and engage with it. We can talk to the energy of anything.

Say your car starts acting up, or your house begins to fall apart, or your plants suddenly droop for no apparent reason; you can ask them, "Hey, what's up? Do I need to do something different here? Or do something differently?

Do you want more attention? Do you want to go to someone else? How can we contribute to each other and flourish together?"

After asking each question, wait for a moment. The first thought that comes up is usually your intuition talking. It's your Awareness. The trick here is to wait for only a second or two. After that, your gray cells kick in. You wouldn't want to go there, since that refers to the thinking-and-doing bit. Those thoughts are accompanied with a sticky pressure of performance. Energy "talks" are exhilarating bits of information that help you open up new choices and recognize a different world of possibilities.

There are times I talk to the energy and molecules of my car seat. I request it to adjust and to help me adjust in a manner that would be kinder and comfortable both to my body and the seat. It works wonders. Try it and notice what changes in a second or two after you have asked.

In addition to asking such customized questions, there are four questions that work wonders in any ambiguous situation. These Access powerhouse questions will assist you to get some clarity.

1. What is this?

When you ask this question, don't look for an answer. It is meant to make you aware of all the information that comes to the surface. You can never reiterate this query enough, since each time you ask, a different awareness to the same situation pops up.

"Is this relevant?" is also a good question. Sometimes just by asking this question, the entire situation redimensions itself, and magically you are no longer obsessed with it. It is just a situation, and situations present themselves many times. It is called life. Still, often these situations have no relevance to you or your life. You just get aware of them. And by that, it doesn't mean you have to do something about it, especially if it is not relevant at that time.

2. What do I do with it?

The information to this inquiry may not always be a detailed to-do report of steps to follow. It could just be a subtle, nudging energy, asking you to probe further. If you still are not satisfied with the data that is being presented, keep asking, "What do I do with this information?" See what comes up. Does the issue you are dealing with get clearer somehow? Or does it go away? Repeat it until you believe you have gotten a substantial base to begin with.

3. Can I change it?

Yes, you can! You can change anything. Just by asking these questions, for example, you've already altered the point of view that it is an insurmountable problem. In fact, many times you don't need to take any further action. Not immediately, anyway.

Though this instance may not need action, rest assured that you have set the ball rolling, merely by raising this query to the universe.

Usually however, when you inquire about something, and in return you get a heavy feeling, like that of a block of cement hitting you, it means the reply is a *NO*. If you feel exhilarated with the response, it is a *YES*.

If there is no radical response or even a vague energetic prod approaching, it means this isn't the right time for you to act on it, or it is not relevant to you at the moment. It can also mean that you are missing some information. Keep your eyes, ears, and sensors alert so you can decipher the additional information when the universe sends you. It is easier to do that now, since you have unlocked the conclusion of the problem with the possibility of a question. The universe is rearranging things for you to see magic. Ask this question again after a few minutes, days, or weeks. You may receive a more affirmative response then.

4. How do I change it?
Like the earlier question, you need not take instant action. Asking a barrage of questions is you giving undivided attention to what you desire to change, and communicating the same with the universe. When you do that, your reality manifests faster.

PURPOSE OF QUESTIONS
One of my girlfriends once asked me, "What questions are you talking about? Ask questions about what?" I replied, "Ask questions about everything." Any question is a good question. Let me point out here that "Why am I so stupid?" is not a real question. It is actually a conclusion only being stated like a question. There is already the presumed conclusion that I am stupid. Rather, if you could ask, "What can I do smarter today?," it would open up an array of possibilities that you could choose from.

Throughout the book you will find questions, not necessarily along with a clearing statement. It is to stimulate and bring up that energy, so you have the choice to react to it or allow it to create more for you.

By asking questions, you start the process of exploring possibilities and entering into communication with the universe. When you inquire about an aspect of your life, the molecules around that aspect of your reality get activated. Say you get a cement block feeling when you raise a query to the universe. It signifies that the energies are stuck and there is no decipherable response. It is as if they are saying, "Huh? What? What's that?" Probably they are telling you, "This isn't the right time for the manifestation of the change you're asking for."

The next time you ask the same or similar questions about that topic, you may receive a different energetic response from the universe. That is because your initial questioning, even if it didn't seem to have any effect then, created something: the particles have started rearranging themselves to provide you with the experience you had asked for. That is when you know that the universe and you are cocreating. It is called active waiting. Don't give up—just give the universe some time and ask again later, when you get the impulse to revisit the question.

The more you pay attention to what you are perceiving by asking different questions, the faster and easier it is to interpret the energies that are communicating with you.

PERCEIVING DIFFERENT ENERGIES

As human beings, there are various kinds of powers we may sense, but either we are unaware of their presence or are inept to articulate our experience.

Since childhood I was perceptive in noticing sensitive energies. As a kid I had two "playmates" (that's what I called them). One I named Buckbuck, and the other was Eddie. They didn't have bodies, and they were invisible to everyone else, but I always knew when they were around.

I also had a recurring dream or image I saw for years. A pale-looking elderly couple, attired in old clothing, would stand at the door of my bedroom and look at me longingly. They never came inside. It was as if they were missing me, so they were calling out to me. I knew they weren't there to harm me, so I never felt scared. But each time it was a gut-wrenching experience because there was nothing I could do about it. I felt helpless since there was no way I could ease their state of being. With time, that image simply faded away.

There were a few more incidents when I witnessed different sorts of energies. Once, on my way back from Milan, as I got off at the train station at Florence I felt the presence of a weird, aggressive force of wind blowing over me. It was whooshing around me at great speed. In reality, though, there wasn't any wind blowing at all.

The next morning when I was on a day trip, I felt the same intense energy at the very same spot. Even after asking many questions, I could not figure out who or what it was, so I let it go. It was not relevant. Many people don't rest unless they get into the thick of such things. In the bargain, they get stuck in a rut. I knew that if I had to know more about it, it would come to me, I had left the question open. If the universe had any information to share that was relevant to me, it would come to me. It didn't, so I let it pass.

A similar incident happened when I was in Costa Rica. I was lying on my bed, relaxing, when out of the blue a tornado of energies started swirling around my room, through my body, and returning in the same pattern. I was stunned. What was going on? After a few minutes, they disappeared as quickly as they had come.

Later, I asked Shannon, an entity expert (people dedicated to understanding the spirit world), what her take was on this incident. She casually asked, "Is it simply that you are more sensitive now to perceiving these energies?"

It isn't that all energies are similar in nature. Some of them are destructive too. I remember that when I had gone to Munich to conduct an Access three-day Body workshop, I had a strange experience. The night prior to my class, when I was in my hotel room, I felt energies whizzing around me. This time I felt scared because they were heavy, destructive, and menacing. They were there to interfere with me in a distracting manner. Thankfully, when I commanded them to go, they did.

Again when I spoke to another entity expert the next morning, she suggested I simply expand my zone and allow myself to receive more information from them. This is one of the communicative tools I teach in my 7steps to Flawless Communication workshops (it is also a book I have authored by the same name).

When you feel heavy, scared, or entrapped, begin expanding the walls of entrapment around you until they fall down flat and you have no barriers between you and all the molecules that surround your body. Keep imagining the space inside you getting bigger until it has gotten bigger than your body, the room, the building, the area, the country, the universe. You'll feel the contracted energies getting smaller.

You can also envision bright light surrounding you completely. Be the light if you can. Light always outshines darkness. Ask all light, positive, contributive energies to make themselves as apparent as these destructive energies. Call on whomever you believe in—Allah, Buddha, Jesus . . . Make the light energies so apparent that the heavy ones get engulfed in them. Repeat this method until you feel the destructive energies have completely diminished.

With this demand in my consciousness, on the second night in Munich when I encountered the caustic energies again, in a stern tone I shouted, "NO. GET OUT OF HERE!," and expanded my zone so great that there was nothing but light in my reality. They never exasperated me again.

When I shared this incident with Gary Douglas, the founder of Access Consciousness, he asked me, "What is being called upon for you that you aren't recognizing? What are you being asked to step up into? Who are you trying to be now?" As I pondered deeper, a whole lot of possibilities flashed before me. Thank you, Gary!

If we allow ourselves to be receptive to receiving all sorts of energies, we can communicate or understand the presence of our loved ones too. For instance, there have been moments when I've felt the presence of Mom even after she had passed away.

Once when I was vacationing in South Africa, after dinner, as I stepped out on the porch for a smoke, I felt a strange feeling. When I proceed from a well-lit place to a dark zone, I get more blinded by that contrast than people usually do. That is the reason I can never see stars in the sky. But this time it was different. For some strange reason I felt an energetic nudge to look up. When I did, I saw millions of stars and constellations moving. Wow! It was mesmerizing. Suddenly the entire thing just disappeared. My mom came into my awareness. I asked her, "Is this you showing me these beautiful creations?" And there they were again! I stood speechless.

All excited to chat with Mom, I asked her to show me more "magic." But it seemed as if she wasn't interested in that. When I was being the energy, she was keen to stay in touch. The moment my mind came into play, she disappeared.

A couple of years later, in South Africa again, when I was on a safari ride, looking to see wild animals, all I could see were birds. Suddenly it struck me that I was sighting lots and lots of birds even before anyone else could lay their eyes on them. I said to my friend Bret, who was on the safari ride with me, "Oh, my mom would have loved to be here. She adored birds. She used to talk to them." He instantly asked me if I felt her presence. When I delved into the energy of that question, there was a drastic change in the energy field of my body. I felt light like a bird, smiling for no apparent reason, and completely relaxed. I turned to Bret and answered, "Yes, she is."

THE POWER OF TRUTH

A complete contrast to Dad, Mom was a thorough social being. Extremely friendly, she loved people. She loved to laugh, sing, dance, and have a good time. Working as a nurse in the pediatric department of a health clinic, she diligently looked after all the kids. She was warm and considerate, and everyone adored her. She loved hosting parties; she was excellent at it. Not much of a drinker herself, she was mostly surrounded by those who loved to booze and have fun.

Generally, she was an easy person to be with. However, she was very particular about a few things—no wasting food, being responsible for one's actions, and speaking the truth, no matter what.

That's my reality too. I could never be dishonest, no matter what price I would have to pay. Even as a teenager, I was open about what I was doing—damn the consequences.

I was living in a place considered the hood. It was like the ghetto in European cities: neighborhoods initially inhabited by Jewish people who later moved out when they started making more money. Later, those areas were dominated by refugees and newly marginalized populations. I was dating one such cool, hip guy from Puerto Rico. He was very cute, and I liked him a lot. Once he had gotten arrested for stealing a car. I wanted to go to court to support him. Most kids my age (I was fifteen at the time) would lie to skip school. While I knew I wanted to be with my boyfriend then, I also knew I would never lie to my mother. I didn't want to lie to my school either. I called my mom when she was working at the clinic, and informed her about me not going to school that day, and I shared the reason for it too. Initially she was livid with me, then moved to tears, but eventually she appreciated my honesty.

I have been a straightforward person all my life. For me, lying has always been much too difficult, because then I would always have to remember that lie. Since childhood, I didn't want to add to my already self-conscious behavior. Speaking the truth came easiest to me.

However, here I must add that down through the years, one of the best pieces of advice I got from my dear friend and college buddy Lesly, a psychiatrist by trade and an earth mother at heart, was "Kass, you don't have to tell the truth about everything to everyone, especially when they haven't asked for it." Wow. Somehow, the way she said it, I actually got that sometimes the kindest thing to do is tell the person only what they can hear, and not to share your detailed truth with them. Thanks, Dr. Baugh!

What have you misidentified and misapplied as being honest that is actually being mean and unkind to others? A truth that does not contribute or add to anything, and only makes people feel bad, is often better left unspoken.

What if we didn't have a fixed point of view about people lying? Have you ever thought of that possibility? If it isn't relevant to you or that individual, do you need to correct it or even address it? Does your need to be righteous or for the urgency for the truth to be known under all circumstances have to be more important than your happiness and the happiness of those around you? What is more important to you—being right or being happy? When you are confused about what to do, simply ask these questions: "Do I really need to say this? Will it be a contribution to that person? Is it even relevant and important enough to bring this up? Will it help the situation if I blurt out my truth here?

TRUTH OF THE MATTER

Speaking of being honest, one of the most potent methods of knowing the truth of a situation, or asking for clarity, is adding the word *Truth* before any question you ask, to yourself, the universe, or someone else. For example, if you are confused about whether or not you should go to a particular place, utter: "Truth, should I go?"

When you ask this question, attaching "Truth" with it, the energy of it is taking into consideration all aspects of the circumstance that you may not be consciously aware of at that moment. Your body will either give you a "yes" (your chest will open up, and you'll feel light, relaxed, and slightly happy too), or it will respond in a way that will make you feel weary, bored, or even sad. It is one of the most effective laws of the universe.

Using this technique, you can also detect if someone is lying to you. Say, you wonder if your business associate is being truthful to you. Mutter "Truth" under your breath (simply saying it in your head is also as effective) and ask that person a direct question. The energy of the answer will immediately inform you of that individual's reality. That is because the utterance of "Truth" creates a field wherein only what is authentic prevails.

Here are a few examples of the kind of questions you can ask to get more clarity:

Truth, am I honoring myself with this choice?
Truth, should I invest in this business?
Truth, will taking up this job be the best choice for me now?
Truth, should I give this relationship another shot?
Truth, is it time to bless this bond and release it?
Truth, should I buy this outfit?
Truth, is this food good for my body?

You can ask questions about any topic and get transparency about the situation.

A lady who was participant in one of my workshops shared with us how this tool benefited her immensely. After preparing a presentation or proposal, she would ask, "Truth, will this client like my offer? Truth, will they be willing to spend their money with me?" Depending on the energetic response she would receive, she would act accordingly. She said she was never wrong with it.

The universe really works with and for you if you are willing to engage it. Everything that doesn't allow you to be willing to look at more options to choose from, times a godzillion, will you destroy and uncreate it all now, please? Right and Wrong, Good and Bad, POD and POC, All 9, Shorts, Boys, and Beyonds.

THE ILLOGICALITY OF BEING

There are periods in life when you need no tool, no technique, no method to offer you clarity. You simply KNOW. How you do, you don't know, but you do. Learning French and leaving Boston were two such confirmations in my life.

When I was eight, studying in the third grade, one of my school teachers, an Irish American woman, would write "Good morning. Today is Monday (the day of the week)" in French, every single day. She did this for the entire academic year. Strangely, I loved that exercise every day. I looked forward to her writings. There was no logical explanation for it, but I always felt deeply connected to that language. In my heart (even at eight), I knew I would be fluent in French someday.

Early on in life, I wanted to get out of Boston because I found both the weather and the people residing there to be cold. My future in my hometown looked bleak to me. Stuck in that trap could never be my reality. I wanted much more for myself.

As a teenager, there were times when I desperately wanted to leave the hood. Just leave it all and run away. The relationships I was in did not excite me. Jobs didn't entice me. But I knew I could never just run away. My dad was huge on education, so I was sure I would have to complete college.

When you are this confident of a particular reality you want, no matter which stage of life you are in, just start acting on it.

Because I would never let down my dad, I decided I would apply to colleges outside Boston. In this manner, I would be able to accomplish both my dreams—finish my studies and be out of Boston—at the same time. Besides applying to Harvard (because that is arguably one of the best colleges in the world), I applied to a couple of other Ivy League schools and New York University business school.

I went to NYU (New York University), where they had an excellent "studies abroad" program. At age twenty, I went to Paris for a year and learned French. I reluctantly returned to New York to complete my studies and stayed on for another ten years. A degree, career, and marriage later, I eventually returned to Europe and settled in Rome, Italy. Today, apart from English, thus far I'm fluent in French and Italian and speak decent Spanish too. I also have what I call "bullshit ability" in a few other languages, meaning I know several expressions and understand bits and parts of those languages too. And I know how to say "hello" and "thank you" in lots of different languages, such as Korean, Japanese, Chinese, Hindi, Arabic, German, Russian, Finnish, Portuguese, and a few more.

DECODING THE SELF

Who am I really?

This is one of the most complex questions ever asked.

In terms of our two-dimensional reality, I am the collaborative manifestation of multiple factors that have influenced me over *Time* and *Space*. Many conditions, situations, and individuals have been instrumental in formulating me. My family, friends, childhood, partner(s) . . . all form a part of who I have become.

Then again, I am the result of all my points of view, which is my reality. My Self is the Ego, or projection of who I am. That is different from me, the Being. I often wonder—is my Self the same as me? My Self is the one who shows up in this reality, while Me is the Spirit, the eternal Being that is connected with everyone and everything and all things. I am the amalgamation of both.

Truth is, I am a conscious being—ever changing and ever evolving. Hence, at any given point in time, the answer to the question "Who am I really?" will always keep varying.

This is the truth of life—following the Energy, constantly evolving, taking baby steps toward knowing the real you; getting closer to your authentic Being. And in this journey, there are no right or wrong paths, decisions, choices . . . there are no good or bad experiences. There is only *Information* that we get (or don't get) from all the experiences we go through. It is all about your points of view about that particular incident or situation. It is these points of view that create the reality you experience. Changing these points of view will change the way you live your life.

CHAPTER 2:

In Communion with Body: From Monologue to Dialogue

"Hi, my name is Toni."

I had renamed myself in high school. I was tired of being called "Kass with the big, fat ass." To me, Toni seemed like a unisex name. More importantly, it didn't rhyme with ass.

I was deeply affected by my schoolmates' judgments. Shocked, really. Traumatized. Their lack of kindness and caring, and those lies resided in my body for many years to come.

CONFINED IN A "CELL"

How can mere "immature declarations" and thoughtless gestures of people have such detrimental consequences on us over long durations?

When we get offended by a judgment (which is a thought, a fixed point of view [POV]), it gets locked in our body. If we choose to hear it and not go into reaction, it can change the effect judgments have on our life. The biological explanation to this occurrence is that

Our body has thousands and thousands of nerve cells.
When we receive a judgment, these nerve cells get electrochemically charged.
Each cell has many thousands of receptors.
Every single receptor has a specific peptide (or protein) attributed to it.
Each individual emotion that we feel releases its oriented bursts of neuropeptides. Say, we are emoting anger. Its neuropeptides flood our body and connect with those receptors that change the structure of each cell.

When cells divide, the new cells take on the orientation of the predominant neuropeptide. Suppose we keep feeling anger for a long time; our body gets filled with those receptors.

Unfortunately, since the quantity of those anger receptors increases exponentially, even if we feel good occasionally, the receptor cells of that new emotion are so few that they are unable to override the previously existing one (in this case, the anger receptors).

The beauty of this is that we can change the equation at any moment. When we CHOOSE to feel different—say, we choose to feel happy— the happy receptors start to grow. That is when our reality starts to shift. The happier we feel, the more such receptors are produced, eventually eradicating anger from our body.

Nothing is permanent. Every molecule in our body is constantly giving us information. If we are willing to receive it, the cellular structure starts to change accordingly.

IT IS LIGHT. IT IS HEAVY.

As we start to pay attention and understand the language our body speaks, we actually cocreate a healthier, fitter, well-balanced body. If something is right for it, we feel light. If it is not, the heavy feeling does not betray us and therefore does not leave us.

If you're gripped in ambiguity, the *Truth exercise* is a good one to try here. Here are a few questions that can help you gain clarity when things are ambiguous:

Truth, Body, is this the right food for you at this moment?
Truth, Body, may I do an extra push-up? Will it be all right with you?
Truth, Body, will you be fine if I stayed up a little longer and finished working on this assignment?
Truth, Body, will going to the beach be a rejuvenating experience for you today?
Truth, Body, would you like to go for a swim?
Truth, Body, is it a good idea to go on this trip?

To better understand the concept of *Light and Heavy*, let's play a game:
Think of someone you really love, and who feels the same way about you. Stay with these thoughts for a few moments.

(Note to self: If you dislike everyone and believe that all hate you, think of anything you are fond of—a pet, a film, a flower, a book, a place, a piece of heaven on earth—that you know or hope exists.)

Once you have recognized that one person/thing you love, utter the following sentence, and check how you feel immediately after, and how your body reacts to it.

Say out loud, "I really hate you."

Are you able to spot the sensations that come up for you? Is there an initial resistance to uttering words you know are untrue? Do you catch yourself feeling or saying, "I will not say that since it simply is not true! This is NOT how I feel"? Or are you so much in resistance, wound up so tight, that you are not even being able to play the game?

If you need to, repeat it a few times and perceive what comes up—in your head, heart, body, universe.

Everywhere that you are in so much resistance to something or someone, wound up so tight that you are not even willing to play, times a godzillion, will you destroy and uncreate it all now, please? Right and Wrong, Good and Bad, POD and POC, All 9, Shorts, Boys, and Beyonds.

Everything that doesn't allow you to look inward and tap into the sensations that your body is giving you and receive the information, times a godzillion, will you destroy and uncreate it all now, please? Right and Wrong, Good and Bad, POD and POC, All 9, Shorts, Boys, and Beyonds.

Second part of the game (get ready to play!):

Repeat the above exercise. Think of someone or something you love and enjoy, only this time, mention how you really feel.

Declare aloud: "I really love you."

This is obviously a true statement. How does it make you feel? Does it feel like it has set you free? Like there is no resistance or contraction in your body? Observe the reaction in your throat, chest, solar plexus, shoulders, stomach, or anywhere you feel a little reaction in your body.

By noticing such sensations in your body, you will be able to comprehend what your body is telling you. When you are able to interpret its messages without a point of view, you will witness a radical transformation in the way you think and perceive your body. This process will make your life much easier and make your options much clearer.

To get well versed with these concepts, try out this exercise using different statements. Love chocolate? Try saying, "Chocolate is yummy." Then, "Chocolate is gross." Hate cold weather? Declare, "Being out in the cold is fun!" Then, "Being out in the cold sucks big time."

Do you notice any difference in your body when you declare the two different statements above? Do the sensations in your body, your heart rate, your breathing, remain exactly the same? Your body will always let you know when something is true or right for you, and when it is heavy and a lie. You just have to ask and be willing to receive the information.

THE MONOPOLY OF MONOLOGUE

To ask my body what it wanted was an alien concept to me. At first, I could not perceive this method. All my life I had been dictating to my body what it should do for me. To constitute a dialogue with it, to take the effort to understand this "foreign" language, and finally to listen to its desires seemed too far-fetched a possibility. It wasn't until I began playing with the *Light/Heavy* tool that I realized how powerful this exercise was.

Once I started applying this technique to everything—what food to eat, outfit to wear, activity to do, etc.—life got much simpler and more fun! Within no time, I also began asking my body for assistance in accessing my awareness. The information I started receiving blew me away. There were times when it went beyond my cognitive ability to comprehend what was happening. It was as if the responses were coming from collective consciousness (from the universe). This broke the tyranny of monologue with my body. A dialogue was always more fulfilling and, again, more fun.

IN NEGOTIATION

I started to notice that the times I didn't ask my body questions or avoided having a dialogue with it, I ended up having a conversation with my body, anyway. If I presumed I already knew the answers, or if I didn't want to hear what my body had to say, somehow, relevant questions would start to pop in my mind, automatically. I could pretend I had nothing to choose from, but deep down inside I knew that was a lie. My stubborn mind had already decided my approach (where I was going and with whom, what I was going to do, wear, eat). I didn't want any new information to alter my plan. Funny, huh?

One classic example of this monologue-dialogue concept is sex, because sometimes we choose partners whom our body has a point of view about, yet we choose to ignore its say. The body can sense when they are not going to be a contribution to us. They may not be kind, they may not receive us well, they may judge us, or it may even be rough for us. However, sometimes we are so attracted to them intellectually that we don't even want to know what our body knows. We are hell-bent on listening to our mind. We have already decided the answer (that the person is going to be good for us).

Everywhere that we are not including our body in decisions that regard our body, such as whom to sleep with, let's destroy and uncreate it all now, please? Right and Wrong, Good and Bad, POD and POC, All 9, Shorts, Boys, and Beyonds.

Everywhere that we have decided that additional information and awareness is not desired or required or is too much, times a godzillion, let's destroy and uncreate it all now, please? Right and Wrong, Good and Bad, POD and POC, All 9, Shorts, Boys, and Beyonds.

Everywhere that we have decided that additional information or more awareness about something means we are obliged to act upon that data (something we would rather not do), and therefore it is better to block it out, times a godzillion, let's destroy and uncreate it all now, please? Right and Wrong, Good and Bad, POD and POC, All 9, Shorts, Boys, and Beyonds.

What if we could negotiate a solution that worked for both, our body and us? When we ask a question and are willing to receive the energetic information or response of it, we can always change the energy of it. We just have to be willing to ask another question with no point of view attached. What if we always had a choice?

What question are we unwilling to ask because we have already decided we know the answer? Everything that is times a godzillion, let's destroy and uncreate it all now, please? Right and Wrong, Good and Bad, POD and POC, All 9, Shorts, Boys, and Beyonds.

What question are we unwilling to ask because we are afraid that the answer may be different from what we have already decided we don't want to do? Everywhere that we are unwilling to receive new information because it conflicts with what we have already decided to be true, times a godzillion, let's destroy and uncreate it all now, please? Right and Wrong, Good and Bad, POD and POC, All 9, Shorts, Boys, and Beyonds.

PICO UNIVERSE—THE UNREAL TRUTH

This is an expression that was coined in Access Consciousness many years back. It means a small universe. A dwelling in our mind that actively churns out fictional fibs about a particular incident.

For instance, when the bullies in my school had given me that nasty nickname, over the years there were thousands of situations I had conjured, believing that premise was true. Such as, before going to a party, I would wonder what people would think had I worn a short outfit? Or I would refrain from enjoying a rich, scrumptious meal for fear of adding a few more pounds.

Those judgments they made about me and my body were furthest from the truth, yet for years I had battered my body and mind over them.

In another case, when I was working with an unbelievably horrible lady for a film festival, I had build up scenarios to "protect" myself. The day wouldn't have even begun, but I would be armed with replies. There were innumerable times when the situations I had anticipated (and had prepared myself to face) wouldn't come to fruition at all. She would get worked up about something else altogether (one that I was not prepared to face), but the damage to my body had already been done, thanks to my extensive travels to the Pico Universe.

If we could visit those Pico Universes a lot less often, and spend more time creating in the present, it would be more of a contribution to our lives, and we would build a better future for ourselves. There are multiple things we can do to minimize mind chatter and get out of the Pico Universes. Get a hobby, for example. Engage in doing something creative. Contribute to ourselves and the environment. Anything that enhances our well-being and keeps us moving forward instead of building false ladders in invisible houses.

MIND CHATTER—GONE WITH THE WIND

We all have blocks of moments when the mind goes into a frenzy, setting foot in Pico Universes, or even worrying about the future. For a major chunk of my life, I had dual citizenship in both spaces.

To share an example: When I was working for the film festival I mentioned above, I would travel by bus to reach the office. It was a daily ritual to lose myself in the universe of each and every passenger, convinced that they too were thinking about me. "Were they judging the dress I'm wearing?" "Did they think my hairstyle wasn't suiting me?" "If that guy (who's staring at me with lust in his eyes) says something crude to me, I'll reply in this tone." A zillion of them. We have all been there, haven't we?

One of the best gifts I received from Access Consciousness at that time was its long verbal processes in the form of questions, followed by the Clearing Statement. It was suggested that I repeat a bunch of them daily, thirty times each. Being a diligent student all my life, I had written them on a piece of paper. I gathered that it was a much more valuable task to engage in than driving myself ballistic by cooking up stories. Each day I would travel, reciting and repeating those verbal processes in my head. I had grown to like the activity. Those long questions left me with no time to buy or invent other realities, other universes.

I remember that one of them was the following: *Perceive, know, be, and receive what I refuse, dare not, must never, and must also perceive, know, be, and receive that will allow me to perceive, know, be, and receive everything I truly perceive, know, be, and receive, and everything that doesn't allow that, times a godzillion, I now destroy and uncreate it all. Right and Wrong, Good and Bad, POD and POC, All 9, Shorts, Boys, and Beyonds.*

This Clearing Statement was about opening our receiving to everything. There were a few others of this kind.

One day I forgot to carry my sheet of verbal processes and questions. For the perfectionist I always was, it was strange that this hadn't frazzled me. Everything seemed to be in synchrony. When I got off the bus, I realized it was quiet in my head. What had just happened? I hadn't gotten into anyone else's universe. It was a wonderfully pleasant ride. It was at that moment that I consciously understood what mind chatter truly was.

CRUISING ON THE AXIS OF COMFORTABILITY

Access Consciousness changed my life fundamentally. From altering my perception of the body to empowering me with tools to create the reality of my choice, life hasn't been the same since.

One of the most radical transformations was breathing the air of comfortability with everything, no matter what the situation was. I stopped worrying and started living. Years back, when I had moved to Italy, I didn't have a high opinion of my body. I was emancipated then—a fact I realized afterward. After practicing the tools, I actually gained some weight.

The other aspect that got drastically modified was that I became comfortable in my skin. Earlier, I would get self-conscious each time I would show my body. I had always been a voluptuous, charming kid, but as I had started getting too much unwanted attention, I would wear clothes that would hide my big breasts. Not anymore. After Access, I started wearing shorter outfits, feeling comfortable about flaunting my body, and my body felt better too.

THE LANGUAGE OF TRUE COMMUNION

Now that I had started having a dialogue with my body and had gotten more comfortable with my sexuality, I presumed that I had accomplished the task of understanding it completely. To add to this, I had also completed a course on body processes. The three-day Access Body course helped me release many barriers I had unknowingly put up against mean people, negativity, and verbal attacks. Now, I felt no contractions, or so I thought.

Once when I was in a session with Dr. Dain (Dain Heer is the cocreator of Access Consciousness), I had a unique experience. As I lay on a massage table for him to run a body process on me, he tried to connect with me, the being, and my body, but in vain. Since he couldn't, I tried to intervene to help him out. To my surprise, even upon my request, I could not get myself to open up to receiving. Emotionally, I felt a complete disconnect with myself. I couldn't reach my core being.

Dain kept trying to help me get in touch with me and connect with my body, but everything seemed to fail. He said, "You are the first person to start Access Consciousness in Europe. You do a lot of this work, yet you're not just about this alone. There is so much more to you than what you do. The best part is that you're a free spirit. You're friendly, sociable, sensitive, and intuitive. There is no need for you to worry about what's going on here. It will come to you."

He asked me to sit up and he sat beside me, held my hand, and addressed the audience: "Kass and I both know this session was over five minutes after it had started. She had shut herself from receiving." When I got off the massage table and was returning to my seat, it felt like a whole different world for me.

If something like this would have happened in the past, I would have been all wound up. Under normal circumstances, I would have chosen **Door 1**: "Oh my God, if word leaked out, what would people think of me? How can I, an Access Consciousness facilitator, not be able to receive? If people got to know about this, what would they think? They would probably not want to come to me at all." But strangely, that mind chatter was absent.

In the past, I may have even gone for **Door 2**: "This was an interesting session." And I would never have thought about it again.

However, here I was left with just one choice: **Door 3**: "No matter what it takes, this is changing, and it is changing NOW." "I WOULD NOT LET MY LIFE BE LIKE THIS ANYMORE." That was my demand on me. "I'll do whatever it takes to change this. Now, universe, help me out here. Show me what I have to do to change this situation, please?" (The concept of **Doors** is explained in detail in chapter 1.)

From that point on, I kept delving deeper and deeper into knowing myself better. I remember that while hosting a body class once, a level of vulnerability showed up in me. I felt this flutter in my solar plexus. "What is that?" I wondered. It was me getting in touch with myself. It was me perceiving my energetic field. I got present to my body. I got aware of the information my body was giving me about energy and movement in it. After that experience, I felt extremely light. From then on, I got this ability to perceive subtle energies too.

Whenever I had a body process run on me after that, I could feel all the energies. I felt completely rejuvenated. The person who ran the process on me started patting himself on his back and saying how good he was at this. To that I replied, "Yeah, you are good and you can be as good as you want, but if I am not able to receive, it's not the same. This time I was able to open up and receive more, and for that I am grateful to me and my body." Going forward, whenever I would get out of my head and I would allow myself to be present with my body, miracles showed up.

SEX IS ABOUT RECEIVING

Talking of receiving, Access Consciousness taught me the true essence of **Sex**. It isn't confined to intercourse. **Sex** is about looking and feeling good about ourselves. Walking tall and strutting our stuff. Willing to receive admiration from others. Recognizing and acknowledging the gift we are to this world.

Self-criticism and hatred toward the body are two of the most common forms of abuse I have seen in people across the globe. Doubting and criticizing oneself and regretting the things one has done in the past also rank high on the list of self-cruelty. Believe me when I say this, since I have met tens of thousands of people around the globe while conducting Access Consciousness classes and my courses on *7steps to Flawless Communication*. It seems to be a universal issue prevalent across cultures, countries, color, and creed.

Whenever you catch yourself doing this, understand you are going to a Pico Universe. Beating yourself up for things that did not work out then can in no way be more valuable than working on creating a brighter future now.

There may be moments when no matter how hard you try to live in the moment, it feels as though that is a distant possibility. Don't worry. Don't get more frustrated and angry with yourself. Live in ten-second increments. This is one of the best techniques I have grabbed from the tool kit of Access Consciousness. Every ten seconds, try to treat yourself better. If you have failed this time, know that if you choose it, you can change your point of view in the next ten seconds. Or the next. Or the next. In this manner, you are inviting a possibility of lowering your anger, rage, fear, or hate at any given moment.

CLEAR THE CHARGE (OF A WORD/THOUGHT)

If practicing the *ten-second-increment* method is not easy for you, another technique, for getting out of judgment and having a Zen state of being, is when you are able to be neutral about any word, thought, or deed. There is a stark difference between being neutral and being indifferent. When you have no fixed point of view about anything, know that it is contributing to your personal growth manifold. Meaning, no energy comes up around it—no resistance, no reaction, no strong agreement or alignment. Nothing but mere information. That is what you have to aim to attain. On the other hand, indifference is when you don't care about what is going on. There is a certain unawareness attached to indifference. But when you are neutral about something, you are well aware of what is going on. You are consciously choosing to have no point of view about the situation or person.

Easy to say, right? Well, you can become nonjudgmental by taking baby steps:

1. Identify what you resist or react to, align and agree with or ignore; what puts you on the defense or gets you on a roll.
2. Recognize how your body reacts when you have a judgment or a fixed point of view about something; when there is a "charge." All of these are "reactive entrapments."
3. Acknowledge that releasing this habit of labeling is imperative to create a new, expansive dialogue between you and your body.
4. Try this simple exercise: repeat the word *Expand—Expand, Expand, Expand, Expand* .. until the charge dissipates.

IN SYNC WITH JUDGMENTS

There are a few aspects in life that you may have tried being nonjudgmental about, but nothing seemed to work. It isn't always about being disapproving or neutral. It is about being honest and authentic with yourself.

During my teen years, no matter what I did, I wasn't comfortable with my teeth. One aspect of it was that they were big, and the other was that a front tooth had chipped when I had fallen down at age eleven. That created a gap between the two front teeth. Though I would love to smile, I barely did because I was too conscious of the gap. In my early twenties, I got my teeth redone, got caps put on, and got the gap closed. Now, though my teeth are big, I am comfortable smiling. And I do that a lot.

I am not big on diets, but if I saw that I was putting on weight and couldn't seem to stop, I would negotiate with my body and find the right diet to fit both my point of view and my body's desires.

Who decides what will make you happy? You do. You choose the points of view you want to work on, select the ones you want to keep, and throw out those that don't work for you. Such as, my teeth were bothering me a lot, I took action to mend the matter, and I am glad I did that.

There are a few social beliefs I don't mind following. For example, I will never choose to wear a pair of torn jeans to a formal meeting. I will wear a conventional outfit for it. It is not about me being a follower of norms. It is not about me respecting the points of view of others. Do I judge someone if they show up in torn jeans? Nah, not at all. It is just something I CHOOSE not to do. If people judge me for being too formal, too Bostonian, I am okay with that, now.

There was a time in my life when I used to feel we give hair too much importance. I would call it "misplaced vanity." I believed that people gave too much attention to what kind of hair someone had or didn't have. I was definitely in resistance to that point of view. At one point, my family would discuss it extensively. So much so that when the "hair discussion" was over, I would ask if we could now have a real conversation. I was always feisty. Earlier, I would wonder if that was the right way to be. Now, I have fun being that way.

Coming back to talking about hair, I realized later that this was one of the many attributes people used to try to fit in. In my course on *7steps to Flawless Communication*, I talk about the numerous veils we wear to adapt to a situation. What is the mask or veil that will allow you to reach out to people? Your hairstyle (a physical attribute) or your attitude or your demeanor . . . whatever that may be, once they have connected with you, you can remove the mask and be your authentic self.

BEING VITAL VS. MAKING VITAL

As a society, we pay more attention to external factors to keep us happy. In the bargain, we lose out on actually being happy with who we really are. We make a particular attribute vital, give it immense importance, and live our lives by that judgment. For example, if we believe we have never to weigh more than x pounds, we push our bodies to exhaustion to maintain that range.

Suppose our body is feeling happy and rejuvenated after sixteen sit-ups, and we don't pay heed to its signal. If the gym instructor has asked us to do twenty, that is what it shall be. Whether or not it is beneficial to our body, who cares? Ironically, our body does.

It is all about perceptions. For many, skin color matters a lot. I never gave this aspect of my body any importance at all. Sometimes, when people ask me if being of color has ever come in the way of my progress, my answer is "I don't know." I never made it vital in my life, so I genuinely would never know if I lost out on a deal thanks to my color. However, I have witnessed it being an issue for others in an indirect way.

At fourteen, at a summer camp, I had met a beautiful girl named Cathy. We kept in touch afterward too. Slowly, we became very good friends. Suddenly, since I had stopped hearing from her, I called at her residence. On the other line was her mom. "Cathy is in the hospital," she said, and banged the phone down on me. I tried calling back to get some more details, but no one answered. I tried again the next day. The automatic operator said the line had been disconnected. I was baffled. What must have happened? I learned later that she was beaten up by the racist kids in her neighborhood for having non-Irish friends and hanging out in my neighborhood. Wow, does all this really exist? How can people have so much judgment about people and places they don't even know?

I told Gary Douglas about this incident (and a few other incidents), and he asked me, "How much are you entering into other people's universes and trying to see through their eyes, to understand how they can have such a narrow point of view?" Perhaps, in my ability to help people change their point of view so they have a broader perspective, I have converted their limited vision to my bad eyesight. Is that why I have what the doctors call tunnel vision? I wonder.

Everywhere that we are reducing our body's capabilities in order to understand someone else's reality or point of view, times a godzillion, let's destroy and uncreate it all now, please? Right and Wrong, Good and Bad, POD and POC, All 9, Shorts, Boys, and Beyonds.

I remember another incident when color did make a difference. Not to me though. It happened in Boston. My childhood friend Andrea and I were chatting away, waiting in line to be seated in a diner. The waitress came forward and asked the guys standing behind us to go to the table. Andrea lost her cool. I genuinely thought the waitress had made a mistake, so I interrupted, "I'm sorry, we were chatting away, so I guess you didn't know if we were ready to be seated. We are." That lady apologized and took us in instead. When we were seated, Andrea articulated her point of view about what had transpired. From her perspective, racism was a norm there. Is it true, or just a point of view?

My mom never made anything about color, culture, or religion significant, so I never understood the concept of giving importance to something where it didn't deserve it. Whether it was art or labeling people or anything, nothing was too vital to her. Everything was included in her world. For instance, it wasn't until I had visited the New York Metropolitan Museum of Art and seen a Picasso painting that I realized we had a small reproduction of it in our living room. Mom never declared, "We have a Picasso painting." When I called her up to tell her I had seen the original in a museum in New York, she said, "Oh, I love Picasso; he is my favorite painter." I had never even heard of Picasso before college. Years later, when I took her to the Picasso Museum in Spain, I had to drag her out of there at closing. That is how much she loved art (but never made a big deal of it).

Another awareness I got when I went to New York was about Jewish names. My writing partner in freshman year in college was a Jewish guy from Israel. I was talking about my mom's good friends to him. When I called them by their names, he interrupted me to say, "Oh, they are Jewish." I had no idea what he was talking about. These women had celebrated every Christmas with us when I was a child. No one had ever mentioned anything about them being Jewish. When I went home for the holidays, I asked Mom about them. She casually retorted, "Oh yes, they celebrate different holidays; that is why they could be with us at home during Christmas." A reality that had never crossed my mind.

All that you have made vital, valuable, and more significant than you, that keeps you in a finite, defined world and stops you and your body from experiencing the ease and amusement of living consciously, times a godzillion, will you destroy and uncreate it all now, please? Right and Wrong, Good and Bad, POD and POC, All 9, Shorts, Boys, and Beyonds.

THE POWER OF A QUESTION. UNQUESTIONABLE.

In Access Consciousness, *Fear* is called a *distractor implant*. Is *Fear* real or is it a lie? When we buy it as real, it distracts us from understanding what is really going on. It doesn't allow us to see the truth. *Fear* separates us from who we truly are. We are unable to live in the present moment. Had we been able to live in the NOW, we could choose or act from the space of being our authentic self.

Once, when I was out with my friends on a trek and some other outdoor activities, *Fear* gripped me as we were crossing a bridge that was at a great height. My whole body contracted. That wasn't me, because I was never scared of heights. I asked, "Who does this belong to? Is it even mine?"

What happens when we ask a question? Within a millisecond of us raising a query, a space of awareness opens up. That is when our body gives us information. If it is a question that gives us a positive perspective, energetically we feel light. If the pressure or contraction that the issue has caused disappears, it means we have actually touched the issue, exposed the lie, and erased its magnetic charge. It feels like the question has neutralized the pressure of the problem. We have hit the bull's-eye.

When I asked whom this belonged to, I saw an image of the bridge across Mexico and Southern California. I saw I was walking on it along with my mother and sister. We, sisters, were on either side of our mother, since she was petrified to look down. She was extremely afraid of heights. Instantly I realized that in an effort to see what was causing her fear, I had entered into her world to see through her eyes. Obviously, I had stayed there for a longer time. In the process, I had limited my vision of how much fun heights can be. My mom's fear of heights had gotten locked in the memory of my body's cells.

To unlock this fear trap, I asked some more questions, did some verbal processes (about being out of control), and used the Clearing Statement. It helped me expand and get more stable. Once I was at ease, I zip-lined. All along while doing this activity, I was petrified. My friends were ragging me in fun, dancing on the platform of the trees. I wanted to kill all of them. At a certain point, there was a huge drop. Had I let fear overpower me and done something stupid, I would never have survived that fall. There was barely a Tarzan kind of rope. I freaked out completely. THIS was the moment I had to survive—either give in to distress, or . . . I started flying in the air, screaming "Tarzan. Jane!" The whole anxiety spell vanished. To push myself further, next, I flew upside down. Nah, no fear.

Let me share another incident: A few months after the "Tarzan" experience, I went on a vacation to Budapest. Along with some local friends, we parked the car in an open space, with all my luggage in it. My friends assured me that it was perfectly safe to leave the car unlocked and go for a local tour. They opened the trunk in broad daylight to get their jackets, and in the process, my luggage got exposed to all who were standing around too. After we returned from our walk, we found my luggage had disappeared. Fear and anger gripped me. I panicked. My experience was similar to the one I had when the fear of heights had consumed me. Like *Fear*, *Anger* is a *distractor implant* too. I immediately repeated the out-of-control verbal processes along with the Clearing Statement, and within no time I was out of fear and anger and was in the space of me again—calm and fun.

How often have you allowed fear or anger or blame or shame to take you out of the present moment and into the strict confines of controlling your life and body? Every time something like this shows up, what if you could take a deep breath, count to ten, reconnect with your body in the process, and choose something different?

FROM MONOLOGUE TO DIALOGUE. FROM DIALOGUE TO THE COMMUNION OF ONENESS.

At the end of it all, what is it that we are all looking for? Peace? Happiness? Good health? Abundance? All of these and many more things. We have access to all of this. The solutions are within us. All of them. We just have to be willing to identify what is it that we truly desire, then ask or demand it for ourselves. Next, we have to be willing to receive the contribution from the universe no matter how it shows up. In the end, acknowledge it when it shows up. What if we could let our body help us get the maximum benefit in this process?

All my life I had been a workaholic. I never knew any other way to be. An immense lot has modified after I learned about the philosophy of being in communion with the body. Respecting its wishes is my first preference now. For example, in case there is an urgent assignment I have to finish, I ask, "Okay, body, this job needs to be done now. Can we do it without you getting ill?" If my body communicates in a manner that says, "No, I can't push myself anymore," I ask more questions. "Okay, can I assign this task to someone else? Can this be executed in a different way so it does not cause physical displeasure?" I keep questioning and listening to my body until I get to a place where both my mind and my body are at ease.

It has been quite a journey—from being a stranger to my own skin to understanding the language of the molecules of my body and uniting with the infinite being that I am. Now, as often as I possibly can, I operate from a space of honoring my body, not letting my mind judge, and celebrating the infinite spirit of my being—a true communion of oneness.

Source of biological study: www.huffingtonpost.com/debbie-hampton/how-your-thoughts-change-your-brain-cells-and-genes_b_9516176.html

CHAPTER 3:

IN AND OUT OF SYNC IN RELATIONSHIPS: LIVING IN ALLOWANCE

I would never have a broken home—a "reality" I thrust upon myself since I was a kid. Both my parents were respectively divorced when they had married each other. I would never follow their footsteps.

At thirty-one, I walked out on my first husband. A couple of years later, we got divorced.

A tall and handsome African American, he was a theater director who matched my *"He was not these . . . list"* quite well. He was not without education. He was not a homophobic. He did not have children from any previous relationships. He did not have an ex-wife. He did not have prejudices about different races, cultures, or languages. He did not hate animals. Fourteen years older than me, he had lived much more of life. This aspect fascinated me. What is more? When I had met him, he could speak French better than I could! Blame it on naivety.

When we love someone blindly, we unknowingly buy all that they speak, hoping that someday they will mean what they say. For instance, he would animatedly talk about us settling in the South of France one day. It took me many years to understand that he was living in a fantasy world. He said he would do *a*, *b*, and *c*, but he never really got proactive about doing any of it. None of his actions demonstrated that he was interested in making those talks a reality.

We live, we learn. Amid the many truths that unraveled after my divorce, as I looked back on my first few decades of life and relationships, one of the biggest clarities I got was that people escaping reality (with drugs, alcohol, or idealistic utopian dreams) were a complete no-no for me. And the other realization was that I don't have to be the only driving force, the main breadwinner, or the only cross-bearer always. (Get off the cross; somebody needs the wood.) And just because someone is intellectually smart and well read, it does not mean that person is smarter than I am.

When I started attending Access Consciousness classes, I would often hear its founder, Gary Douglas, say, "I am dumber than dirt. Dirt is smart; at least it knows in which direction the wind is blowing."

Everywhere that we judge anyone (positively) as smarter than we are, and, therefore, we are willing to override our innate awareness in favor of their intellectual and seemingly rational conclusions, times a godzillion, let's destroy and uncreate it all now, please? Right and Wrong, Good and Bad, POD and POC, All 9, Shorts, Boys, and Beyonds.

JUDGMENT VS. AWARENESS

In my childhood, when Mom would discuss Dad's misdeeds with me, I would cringe. I would think to myself that I would never criticize my husband to anyone. That is not the right thing to do. It dawned on me later (when I was married) that I wasn't being rude if I was sharing my story with someone I was very close to. Actually, I was merely relating an observation I had made about my husband.

I had made "no judging my husband" so prominent and significant that I wasn't willing to look at all the unkind or unconscious things he was doing. Finally, when I got fed up with his behavior and had a conversation with my girlfriend (the only time I did), he overheard me, and he was shocked to learn of all the things about him that annoyed me. So was I. I had not realized that I was feeling that way about him.

THE FINAL STRAW

August 1994 started a six-month period in my life when everything was changing drastically. I got fired from my job. I sued them (something that was totally out of character). One of my closest friends got very ill. He had to be admitted in the hospital. During this time, my (ex-)husband was keen to go on a vacation together. My heart wanted me to be with my ailing friend, but my mind ordered that I play the dutiful wife. My mind won. While I was away, my friend died; my husband seemed unaffected. His meanness and lack of caring (for me) appalled me. But I was responsible for my choices, so why blame him, right?

Our marriage kept deteriorating further. Since I was without a job, my sister-in-love (that is how I now refer to my former sister-in-law) asked if I would like to travel with her to Europe. A jazz vocalist by profession, she was keen for me to handle her work on the road. In February 1995, she and I took off to the different lands in Europe for our musical tour.

In the past, when I had lived in Europe for a year, I had gotten a taste of living a carefree life. To add to those rich experiences, my being on this musical tour, which involved international travel, meeting people from diverse walks of life, handling events—all these exciting experiences altered my perspective of life and my marriage. I got in touch with who I truly was—an adventurous, fun, loving, and carefree individual. The difference between my authentic self and who I had become in my marriage was too stark for me to ignore any further. Once upon a time, I was this bright light. A free spirit. Now, much of that light had dimmed. Diminished, almost. If I needed to survive (forget flourish), I would have to break up that darkness with little dots of light.

After I returned, I made it amply clear to my now-former husband that I was not ever going to take up a conventional job again. He retorted, "Well, one of us would have to do a real job." I had done that for eight years! It was his turn now.

That outburst broke the floodgates of my pent-up anger and frustration. For the first time we had a long conversation about all that was not working in our relationship. When I listed all of them out, he was in total agreement with me. Since we had nothing left in common, I decided to quit this association. He scoffed and said, "People don't just get up and leave, you know." I did, and I never looked back.

When we get back in sync with who we truly are, the dormant strength within us rises and complements us to take our life forward in the right direction. It is not about the actions we need to take. It is a realization—I value myself, so I deserve more than this.

THE STAMP OF COMPLETION

There is an overbearing presence of dense energy in our lives when we try too hard to recover a situation that has passed its prime. It is followed by a moment of ultimate knowing when awareness knocks at our door, yet sometimes we choose to ignore it. We remain living in bondage.

How often do we allow others to dim our light so subtly and continuously that we ignore and eventually forget all about the light that shines within us? Everywhere that we have chosen anything else over our own light, let's destroy and uncreate it all now, please? Times a godzillion. Right and Wrong, Good and Bad, POD and POC, All 9, Shorts, Boys, and Beyonds.

Five months prior to leaving my first marriage behind me, I did a twelve-week course based on a book titled *The Artist's Way* by Julia Cameron. It had a unique methodology, one that taught me to value myself more than anyone else. For the first few weeks I took myself out for lunches, dates, movies . . . During those days, every morning I had to pen my feelings for twenty minutes. Even if I wrote blah, blah, it was all right, but I had to jot down what I was feeling. I wasn't allowed to read my copy for the first eight weeks. Eventually, when I did, I was shocked and embarrassed for myself.

All along, I had not realized that I had been writing the exact same experiences every single day. This helped me assess how miserable I was in my marriage.

We can switch off the lights and pretend it is all dark, but once they are on, there is no hiding behind the shadows of our weaknesses. It is time to come out in the open and shine bright.

BE KIND TO YOURSELF

On one hand, here I was this headstrong Boston girl who had made a life for herself outside her hometown. On the other hand, she was living a lie being married to a man who was not willing to love or care for her; one who was willing to love only himself.

What if trying to be nice were a limitation? My desire to constantly be nice and considerate to him had me working double time. What if, instead, my first priority was to be kind to me? Would being kind and considerate to others be much easier? When you are willing to be kind to you, then it is easier to be of service to others. You then live a life of abundance and become a contribution to everyone and everything in the universe.

TWISTED REALITY

At times, don't we have weird ways of validating our partner's shortcomings? Since he was fighting for a better life for the troubled youth, I believed he was a huge contributor to this world, more than I could ever be. Several of my friends had been fighting for various causes: protecting the environment, educating incarcerated women . . . I was the only one leading a mundane life—going to work and paying bills. Didn't that make me a lesser mortal? No, I realized, after we both went to the tax office.

In an attempt to make our crumbling marriage regain some stability, I thought that if we combined our taxes, he would have a better tax situation. After scrutinizing his papers when the tax officer told him he hadn't paid taxes in ten years, he passionately muttered, "Doesn't it matter that I'm helping the underprivileged youth?" Both the officer and I stood stunned.

A BETTER ME

Failure is a relative term. My divorce educated me that I was not a failure because a particular relationship had not worked out. On the contrary, irrespective of my marital status, I have kept in touch with his family. After all, the intricacy of an intimate human relationship is far more complex than the simplicity of a signature on a dotted line. I'm still in touch with that family, and I continue to give and receive love in those relationships.

What if you always allow yourself to receive the gifts from every situation? What if there are no mistakes, only choices, possibilities, and contributions? What questions can you ask about a seemingly negative situation that would allow you to reap the positive benefits before and after it has occurred? Everywhere that moving on means leaving behind everything—throwing the baby out with the bathwater—believing it is impossible to undo the past, and setting out to prove you are right in believing so, times a godzillion, will you destroy and uncreate it all now, please? Right and Wrong, Good and Bad, POD and POC, All 9, Shorts, Boys, and Beyonds.

Everything that stops you from making an agreement to live your life believing all things are possible, times a godzillion, will you destroy and uncreate it all now, please? Right and Wrong, Good and Bad, POD and POC, All 9, Shorts, Boys, and Beyonds.

THE BEST OPTION

In reality, to modify anything, all we need to do is honestly look at what is. There are many who are unwilling to do that. They invest their creative energy in fixing that which is not working. But is it worth saving it at all? Sometimes it is better to move on.

I held on to my production company for six years when I could have shut it down after I had completed making my film. Most people do that. They open and shut their firms after making a film or two. It is a clean break so they don't have to keep handling problems pertaining to the company or the past. But because I had made closure such a big deal, I kept my company open. I had to deal with all the issues that came along with its lingering presence, yet I chose to keep that part of my life alive and open. The moment I chose to end my relationship with my firm, as I had done with my first marriage, I started making lots more money, and many more possibilities showed up.

If you are finding it tough to take a decision about what to do in a situation, ask these questions:

> *Is this relationship creating more or less in my life?*
> *Truth, is this the best use of my time and energy? Is there something else easier and more in sync with my energy that would create more for me and for everyone else, now and in the future?*
> *Truth, what is my best choice at the moment?*
> *Truth, is it time to bless this situation and release it? (Thank you, Mother Pierce, for that one.)*

These energetically powerful questions are practical and potent tools for change. Once we engage the universe in helping us sort out the situation (which is what we do when we ask questions like these), magic and miracles become part of our reality. How does it get any better than that?

MAKE IT ABOUT YOU

A course I conduct, called 7steps to Abundance, teaches participants to recognize the difference between making a situation work and making life work in a way that suits you best. It is about knowing in your bones what is true for you and respecting your intuitive awareness (rather than living someone else's lies).

In the beginning, it may seem like it is a very tough task, but when we stick our neck out of our limited reality and realize that it is not THE reality, it gets easier to get out of the rat hole. All we need to do is change our point of view and go with the flow of our intuition.

YOU DECIDE

Every relationship has its distinctive dynamics. Following the energy of that flow, keeping in mind the egos at play, is not always a cakewalk. Is it worth all that effort? Who decides? You do.

After my first divorce, I took it easy for a while. Later, through common friends, I ran into Marco again (I had met him years back), my future husband.

It is ironic how my life has been uncannily similar to that of my parents. Like them, Marco and I too were in our respective relationships when we fell in love. We both realized, beyond the shadow of a doubt, that we would be happiest together. I was already in a new relationship and quite content with it. Still, when Marco and I reconnected, it was a completely different experience for me. I had never felt this excited and ecstatic before. My breakup was neither easy nor pretty, but this time, I chose to be kind to myself. I chose to follow my intuition.

Marco traveled to London to break off his relationship. It had not been easygoing for either of us, but it was worth it. We both knew in our hearts we were meant to be together. Today, over two decades later, our love for each other has only strengthened.

This philosophy extends to every kind of relationship. Many times, kids and parents are at constant loggerheads. Why do they need to stay together? Life is too short to walk on a singular, spike-ridden path. If you enjoy being with whom you are now, carry on. But if the journey is more of a constant compromise, then it is time to make a choice and take a decision.

WORTH A SHOT

Marco and I have lived through a lot of challenging experiences, and our love for each other and respect for our individualism have always been a gift.

I have been a workaholic all my life. I may not have been the best organizer of time either. In 2010, there was a phase when Marco wasn't feeling honored enough. He felt I had dedicated my life to my work. We were in a constant state of conflict. We didn't have any idea how to handle it. At one point, he said to me, "Look, the fact that we love one another is not in question, but we cannot die for this relationship."

When he articulated his feelings in this manner, it put a lot of things in perspective for me. It gave me the freedom of choice to be who I wanted to be. I didn't have to defend or pretend. I honored and respected him more for being authentic. I chose our marriage. This time around, the choice to hang in there was the right one for me.

All of us have had to face such turbulent moments in relationships. Asking these questions helps:

> *Truth, what could show up if I were willing to destroy and uncreate all my fixed points of view about having to hold on to something or someone that is not working for me?*
> *Truth, shall I hang in there?*
> *If I hang in there, is this a dead end or just a bump that will ease out in time?*

TO BE OR NOT TO BE

When we are clear about what is important and vital to us, who and what matters to us, things automatically fall in place. It is not a war of egos. Rather, it is a sincere, collective effort to mend the relationship.

Now I have found different ways to include Marco even when I am busy working. No matter how hectic my schedules get, I don't cut him off completely. It is not about calling him every five minutes. Sometimes, when I am traveling, the whole week goes by and we don't talk on the phone. This happens especially if I am in a different time zone from his. But since I keep him in my awareness, my energy keeps flowing his way. This is how energy fields work. When you think of them, they feel your presence even from a distance. Sometimes I talk about him in my classes and workshops, so he is part of my universe even if he is not physically present with me. When I am touring, these little "connections" keep our marriage going.

PERSPECTIVE AND PRIORITY

It is all about these two Ps. Each one of us has our own understanding of how the relationship is, and we operate from that reality – a startling fact I learned at thirty-two, when once I was thinking deeply about my dad. I called him on the phone.

"Hello, Dad. It's me, Kass. I just got present to the fact that though Mom, Kim [sister], and I always believed you were a tough man to live with, it may not have been necessarily true. It probably wasn't that easy for you either. It must have been quite disheartening, living in a house with three women who didn't think too highly of you."

There was silence on the other end. Just a sniffle. After a while he uttered, "I never thought anyone would see it that way."

With that perspective altering, there was a paradigm shift in my awareness. I apologized to him. I hoped he would forgive me someday. We couldn't change the events that had happened in the past, but if we could change our points of view about those events, a lot would shift within us. What else was possible now?

As my point of view about my dad changed, my relationship with him got better. It had a ripple effect. My views about mean people were not the same anymore. All my life I had avoided them. Now, I no longer had any fixed point of view about mean people. I didn't see it as right or wrong. It was just an interesting point of view.

My dad had a very tough childhood. Through the years, his defenses had become his personality. People often develop certain personalities to protect the soft person they are inside. Instead of instantly reacting to the behavior of someone who is snappy, what if we could look past their style of communication and understand what they are truly trying to tell us? What if we could see them without any judgment. It would be the most inviting perspective to have. And maybe, just maybe, then they would come out from behind the walls of defense that they had so carefully built up all their lives. Maybe then they would reveal who they really are.

After the death of his brother Phil, my ex-husband and I no longer made discord the priority in our connection and were finally able to have a harmonious exchange. What a different perspective.

What fixed point of view have you made a priority about someone which does not allow you to perceive them from a different perspective and acknowledge their kindness? Everything that is, times a godzillion, will you now destroy and uncreate it all. Right and Wrong, Good and Bad, POD and POC, All 9, Shorts, Boys, and Beyonds.

INTERESTING POINT OF VIEW

One of the best tools of Access Consciousness, these four words can literally change the mood and energy of any conversation. I invite you to say (or think), "Interesting point of view," every time you get an urge to be all righteous and judgmental about something.

There are ample examples of how this phrase can ease out the set thought patterns of just about anything. For instance, when I went to Ireland I noticed many expressions that began with "Well, we are Irish, you know, so . . ."

What is interesting about this phrase is that it is packed with history and pride. In many ways it is a disclaimer. There is a whole lot of energy that comes up around it, no matter who says it. Energy of the past, the present, the British, the protests, and the suffering. It is hugely entrenched in the psyche of the people. Those six words ("Well, we are Irish, you know . . .") invoke and perpetrate a mentality that has influenced several generations.

What have I made so vital about "being Irish, ya know" (fill in the race, sex, or creed that you align with) that keeps me stuck in that part of history? Everything that is, times a godzillion, I now destroy and uncreate it all. Right and Wrong, Good and Bad, POD and POC, All 9, Shorts, Boys, and Beyonds.

What have I made so vital about being single, married, gay, or straight, or what have I made so vital about being a good friend/lover/husband/wife/father/mother that does not allow me the freedom of choice and that keeps me stuck in someone else's idea of relationships? I now destroy and uncreate it all. Right and Wrong, Good and Bad, POD and POC, All 9, Shorts, Boys, and Beyonds.

BARRIERS: FRIEND OR FOE?

While "Interesting point of view" eases the rigid energy around someone's authoritative declarations, *Barriers* (up or down) play a significant role in how a conversation can be tweaked to suit what is best for us.

Here is an example of a *"Barriers Up"* conversation:

As I was traveling to New York, I decided to meet my old pal there and have a good time. She was in Rome when I had moved in. After she moved back to New York and settled in the States, we had lost touch with each other. All excited to meet her now, I messaged her. She replied, "Listen, you write to me only when you're in New York. At other times, you don't call or bother to keep in touch." To that I replied, "I don't keep in touch with my sister either. Sometimes months go by."

Now raising her barriers higher, she continued, "I'm not talking about your sister here." Putting my barriers down completely, I reapproached the situation. "I may not be good at maintaining the kind of continuity you require in a friendship. I wish I could promise to do that, but that's not possible for me at this moment. I really do adore you and would love to see you. If something changes on my end, and I'm able to do that with more ease, I'll keep you informed. And if ever you don't need that aspect as much, do let me know."

The relationship changed completely. I think of her often. Marco (an architect by profession) even redesigned her house. We have common friends. We hear about each other, but she and I have not been in touch with each other in years.

When you honor the truth of who you are, and do not diminish yourself to fit in a relationship, you have no guilt or remorse.

LET IT GO

The other aspect about putting your barriers down is that when you are open and vulnerable (which does not mean you are weak), people cannot hold onto their judgment(s) about you (or anything else for that matter) for long. When you are willing to receive judgments without any point of view, without resistance, you do not lock it into your body and others cannot lock it into their world either. It's a win-win situation. Play with letting judgments pass through you. Use what you can to learn something (if it helps). If there is nothing in it for you, let it go.

FEELING A BARRIER

Imagine a fortress in a desert. You are standing outside that guarded territory. Exposed on all sides, you can be attacked from any direction, but since you are out in the open, you CHOOSE when you would like to mount your defense, how you would like to mount your defense, and if you would like to defend yourself at all.

Now, imagine if you are inside the fortress. You feel all comfortable without having to worry about being attacked, because people can't see you inside. However, the truth is, you can't see them either. Therefore, you are in a constant state of defense, because you do not know when or from where you would be attacked. When your barriers are up on all sides, you are completely fortified. But who is in prison?

BARRIERS-DOWN EXERCISE

Start with your hands above your head, palms facing the floor, and begin slowly pushing your palms toward the floor.

Slowly.

S-L-O-W-E-R!!!

See if you can perceive the electrical charge all around you. Anytime you feel there is a slight pressure (the barriers are up), ask, "Can I push them down a little bit further?" Do not demand them to go; ask or invite them to go down. As you do this, observe what is going on in your body. As your palms move toward the floor, you simultaneously let the barriers come down.

Go past your forehead, eyes, nose . . . as you push them down, feel the rigidity and the tension getting lower. Stay present with your hands as you move them down in front of you or beside you. Slowly stop if you feel there is a block. If the barriers need a little cajoling, be there, hold on for some more time. Then slowly push them down all the way until they're at your feet. Do this with your entire body.

As you keep repeating this exercise, you will get better with being at ease. Some days may be very good, while other days there may be a few barriers up. Do it without any judgment, to get more information about what is going on in your body and energy field. Eventually, you will realize you are not affected by everything that is happening around you. You will not get flummoxed by anything that anyone says to you, and your conversations and interactions with family, friends, colleagues, partners, and strangers will go a lot more smoothly. You will receive much more.

For all these changes to take place in your life, first you have to be willing to receive information that comes up. If you are cagey about change, you will be in a stalemate situation.

Let me share another example of how it helps us when our barriers are down:

Once when I was lunching with my colleague in Paris, a guy walked up to us and said to me, "Hey, I saw you two months back in Paris, and here you are again. I really don't like the Access bit."

With my barriers slightly high, I thought to myself that here is a stranger who has walked up to me and is sharing his truth—bad-mouthing something without even being asked about anything. Here I am being disturbed in the middle of a meeting; maybe if I lower my barriers completely, it will help me.

Not realizing I was lost in thought, he continued, "I loved the presentations you did on communication skills." Suddenly, he said something in Portuguese; I replied in the same language, and the ice broke between us. In due course of our conversation, he shared how he had many contacts in Brazil, since he had lived there for six years. Wow! I was going to Brazil in the following year in April. We shared our business cards as we said our goodbyes. Had I kept my barriers up, the conversation would not have ever reached this point.

FLOW ENERGY. PULL ENERGY.

Like *Barriers (up or down)* is a play of energies, *Flow and Pull Energy* is a similar exercise. The beauty of these techniques is that any complex situation can be sorted out by using your capacities to engage with the energies of the universe. They are omnipresent. Free. Easy to use. Extremely beneficial. How does it get better than that?

Let's do an exercise:

Think of the last orgasm you had. It could have been this morning, last week, or even a decade ago. If you have never had an orgasm yet, think of the excitement you feel when you do something you love. Think and get the energy of it. Now, pull that energy up from the floor: through your feet; past your ankles, shins, and knees (let it circle around your knees); then through your thighs. Run it through the sexual organs, up through your stomach, chest, and neck. Give your neck and shoulders a nice roll, and let all that energy flow through your shoulders, flow down your arms, and drip from your fingertips.

Now with your hands, pull that energy back—up through your hands, shoulders, and neck and out the top of your head. Stay with it for at least sixty seconds. Allow that energy to flow throughout your body.

This is your orgasmic energy of living. If you perceive it anywhere in your body, such as your shoulder blades, back of your neck, or wherever it is, then send some of this energy to a place in your body that is not receiving it. You will feel energized, excited, and relaxed at the same time.

Take nice, deep breaths.

Let me share an incident here for clearer understanding:

Once, my friend Mike had come to an airport to pick me up. He did not know I had already stepped out, so he kept staring at the exit, waiting to see me come out. His back was facing me. Calling out to him was not possible, since there was a glass partition separating us, so I started pulling energy from him. Real hard. He could feel the difference in the energy around him. He started looking around in all directions. Finally, he looked at me standing outside the window. That is an energy pull. Haven't you ever experienced something like this? Truth?

WHAT IS THE WORD FOR IT?

Since *Energy* is vibratory and so are *Words*, they can be manipulated to deduce the kind of outcome we desire. For example, the use of appreciatory words heals our bodies faster, while criticism has an adverse effect on them.

Whenever we operate from a space of contribution, our worlds expand, creating abundance. Ego separates us. It excludes us into an isolated entity. The words we use to communicate with the universe make all the difference. If we are not getting what we desire, it is time we check the words we are using.

Say that when we assign a task to someone, if we use words that involve them (instead of giving them commands), the outcome will be far more productive. Instead of pointing out their flaws, if our approach is more inclusive, the process and the work benefit all of us. We can ask them if it was fun doing the project. What is it that worked for them? What is it that did not work for them? Do they have suggestions to make such work more enjoyable in the future?

EFFECTIVE COMMUNICATION OR NEED FOR CONCURRENCE

It is interesting to notice how, sometimes, we confuse communicating and concurring with our views as one and the same thing. Earlier, many times, when I would say something to an individual and if the response was not the kind I had expected in return, I would rephrase myself. I would presume the person had not understood me. Once, my cousin Vaughn said, "It's a funny thing—when people don't agree with you, you think it's because they don't get what you are saying, so you keep trying to explain it in a different way, until they get your drift." Probably I thought that if I could not make them see my point of view, I was not being an effective communicator. Now I realize that this is not always the case.

What are we unwilling to perceive, know, be, and receive about the binary encodings and the occlusions of the language that don't allow us to see other people's points of view?

What fixed points of view do we have that don't allow us to see all points of view?

If we are willing to have no fixed points of view, then we can have all points of view and create more ease in our relationships and communication with others.

After I started applying the tools of Access, I got more aware of what people can hear. Now, when I speak from a space of inclusion and creation, I create so much more.

To get more clarity on this, you can ask these questions:

> What is it that I would like to communicate that I am not saying in a way that others can hear it?
> What is it that I have to say that I am not saying, which if I would say it, it would change someone's reality?
> Will saying this make a difference in the world?
> What is the effect I desire to create here?
> What is it that I can say that will make someone uncomfortable enough to stimulate change in the way they look at reality, even if it is just for a moment?

A classic example of the last question is when my ex-husband and I had our long conversation and confronted reality together. As I spoke with him about the things that were not working out in our marriage, I was not merely looking for his approval. I was not trying to convince him either. I was only stating my truth. That changed the course of both our lives.

IN ALLOWANCE

One of my girlfriends, Annie, was in the service of teaching those who are incarcerated to write. Once when we got talking, I had expressed my apprehension about not being able to do what she was doing. Since I was highly sensitive, I would get involved in the reality of those behind bars. Feeling people's pain is not an alien concept to me. To that she replied, "There are those of us who are piercing the darkness with points of light, but we need people like you who continue contributing to the light, so that those in the darkness know there's still light out there somewhere." That meant that my being happy and content with who I was was still a contribution (a truth that changed my reality).

Many people set out to change the whole world, but they somehow manage to keep themselves out of that picture. What if we could change the world by changing ourselves first? We live in this two-dimensional reality: polarity (right and wrong, good and bad, black and white) and oneness (which includes everything, even polarity). What if we were not focused on changing the entire universe, or anyone in particular, for that matter? What if we are in this reality to create a world that best suits us? Funny thing is, when we do that, we automatically change the world.

For those who are looking for a fulfilling relationship, here is what I would suggest you do: work on yourself and find a way to make this world pleasant for you; it will be reflected in the energy that you are. You have to start with you first. That is where it all begins.

CHAPTER 4

THE ENERGY OF MONEY: BEYOND FORM & STRUCTURE

Observe your breathing. As you inhale and exhale a breath, the next one is waiting, ready to roll in. You are not concerned about the availability of your next breath (except in unique cases). Usually it is a seamless and effortless "manifestation".

Air is *Energy*. So is *Money*.

Like *Air*, what if *Money* too could be omnipresent in your life? What if *Money* seamlessly and effortlessly manifested in your life? What if you always had more money than you could ever spend? How would that make you feel?

STEPPING INSIDE THE ENERGY FIELD

Everything is *Energy*—palatable and perceptible. If paid close attention to, it speaks louder than words. In fact, *Energy* is our first language. That is why, when we close our eyes and visualize being surrounded by money, we feel the resounding vibrations of abundance, even in silence.

When I talk about money or riches or wealth, I include words such as currency. In English, currency symbolizes "an ongoing current of energy flowing." It is the variation in frequency of this flow that dictates the extent of wealth that can show up in our lives. The continuity and consistency of this flow determine the ease with which money enters in our lives on a regular basis. The more the flow, the richer we are.

ASK. AND YOU SHALL RECEIVE.

This is literally the case. The more questions we ask, the more we are able to create simply by following the energetic responses we receive. It gives us more possibilities from which to choose.

One of the most potent questions we can ask ourselves is this: *What can I add to my life today that will bring me more money right away? Everything that doesn't allow me to have complete clarity on that, times a godzillion, I now destroy and uncreate it all. Right and Wrong, Good and Bad, POD and POC, All 9, Shorts, Boys, and Beyonds.*

The purpose of asking a question is to obtain information, not necessarily in the form of a conventional answer. Let me explain in detail what I mean by this. When I decided to move to Italy (from New York City), I had planned to take it easy for some time, relax into my new environment, perhaps even write a book. Since I had a nice sum of money set aside in my savings account, this was a luxury I could afford. One day, when I stepped out to soak in the beauty of this new country, I happened to glance upon a gorgeous Italian-style bag. A perfect start to fit in this land's rich fashion culture.

"Sorry, ma'am, you have no cash," the salesperson over the counter stated, handing me back my debit card. That is impossible! "Of course, I have money in my account," I retaliated. Well, almost. How could my transaction have gotten rejected? This was a mistake.

Oops. No, it wasn't.

For him to have a better tax arrangement, I had decided that my husband (later, ex-husband) and I would file our taxes jointly together. Unfortunately when we broke up, he stopped paying his back taxes and since he did not have money in his account to seize, the IRS extracted that from my account. Out of fairness, they had sent me a warning letter stating that if they did not hear from him in two weeks, they would have to seize the money from my account (since we were now paying jointly). The notification was sent to my New York address, but I was not there to receive it. I was in Italy. So, the IRS extracted everything from my account (which was the money I had saved). This was quite an expensive exit plan.

I was in Italy settling in, and now I had no money. Wow! Fortunately, since I was residing in my fiancé's place (who is now my second husband), at least I had a roof over my head.

Needless to say, I was extremely angry with my first husband. When I got in touch with him, he said that he would contact the IRS, and he promised he would pay me back my money. He did neither of these things. I held on to this grudge against my ex-husband for so long that until I let it go, I did not allow myself to make more money than the amount of money I had lost. The moment I got over it, the moment I let go of the idea that "he would have to pay me back the entire amount or else . . . ," my whole financial situation changed. When I became okay with that amount never coming back to me from him, I felt a lot lighter. I recognized that moment because I was able to tell the story without breaking into a sweat and getting all worked up. Energetically, it no longer had a hold over me. Once that happened, I started getting calls for jobs, and, eventually, money started pouring in from known and unknown sources.

What grudge are you holding on to, that if you were to let it go, it would allow you to receive more money? Everywhere that you are allowing a past situation to dictate how much money you can earn and receive, times a godzillion, will you destroy and uncreate it all now, please? Right and Wrong, Good and Bad, POD and POC, All 9, Shorts, Boys, and Beyonds.

Everywhere that you are making a debt—that someone else owes you— more real and valuable than your potential to make more than that, instead of getting over it, times a godzillion, will you destroy and uncreate it all now, please? Right and Wrong, Good and Bad, POD and POC, All 9, Shorts, Boys, and Beyonds.

A participant in one of my workshops was sharing how his brother had owed him money. He was doing extremely well for himself, but he was hung up on getting his money back from his brother. He believed that such things should not happen in a family. That is not how family members should be treated. Little did he realize that by holding onto his rigid judgments about how a particular thing should be, he was stalling more money from flowing into his life.

Clients have often asked me what it will take for that individual to pay them back their money. I have always given them a simple answer: when you lend someone money, be willing to never get it back. Gift it to them, do a trade with them, or don't give it to them at all, but whatever you do, don't put all your energies into waiting in agony to get your money back.

Once things got sorted out in my head, I started asking different questions. Upon doing that, the denseness of the energies started decreasing considerably. Now I could see beyond the anger and the grudge. It ceased to be terrible and dramatic. Even though I did not have much money of my own, the energetic responses I kept receiving were still to take it easy for some time. It will all fall into place. Go with the flow. So, I decided to follow my gut.

I did not rush into another job. I chose to invest in preparing for a more comfortable future in this new land. I gathered that it was best I first learn the native language. For a month I went for intensive lessons in Italian. Simultaneously, I was open to any and every opportunity that the universe offered me. The universe presented a series of options, and then there was an apt opening that felt quite light. I started teaching English to an Italian lady.

Later, the same woman hired me to work with her for an international film festival. In the interim, I also worked at various music festivals. This work arrangement lasted for ten years. I met some amazing people from across the globe and even toured with the noted singer Ray Charles. Also, since I spoke different languages, my experiences with people were varied and richer.

Whatever offers came my way, if they felt light, I said yes to them. I even produced a film for an American guy. I realized that my skills and abilities could be a contribution in many different sectors of the workplace, and I always had work. Eventually, I started making more money than I had lost due to my ex-husband.

GO WITH THE FLOW

As I started asking more and more questions for all kinds of situations, I became acutely aware of the difference: times when I overruled the energetic responses and chose something even though I knew it felt heavy, it backfired. When I went with my energetic guidance system, went with the flow, life was smooth sailing.

Following the energy is not simply about saying yes to anything and everything that is showing up. It is about being the invitation to have different things show up and then asking this question: What is going to create more here? And choosing it! Asking questions that take into consideration the future we desire to manifest offers different possibilities from which we can create more of anything. When we identify which of the choices in front of us is lighter and opt for the one that will create the most, some other possibility shows up. Then we can ask another set of questions about that choice. We can keep doing this exercise until we feel that this is what the best choice is for us right now.

That is what I like most about energy work—its dynamism. There is always something to look for, be curious about, investigate, and understand. And then, ask some more questions. It is stimulating and fun. In this manner, we never get bored, and our understanding of how to continually create by following the flow of energy never stops. The more the flow, the richer we are.

YOU KNOW THAT YOU KNOW

This is a classic example of how following the energy can completely turn around our lives:

A young lady who was working as a secretary at a Waldorf school (in Canada) was content being where she was. One day, a millionaire dropped by her school and was keen to meet the owner. He was interested in buying that school. Being the secretary to the director (who was also the owner) of the school, the lady got aware of this development. When she shared this information with her boss, she realized that he was not interested in selling his school. However, she was of a different opinion. Leaving his business card behind, the potential buyer asked this lady to inform him in case the owner changed his mind.

The lightness of this new prospect had inspired the lady considerably. Something about this felt right, but there was nothing she could do, since the owner was rigid. When she called the buyer to inform him about the owner's final decision, the two got talking. She expressed her interest in the project and left it at that.

Within a short period, when this businessman bought another Waldorf school, this lady joined him. Her operational and managerial skills helped that school flourish exponentially. Later, she bought the school. In time, she sold it for over a million dollars, invested that money elsewhere, and started other businesses. Cathy Sawyer is a millionaire now. From a secretary to an owner of various businesses—how does it get any better than that?

Many people can't even bring themselves to say "multimillionaire"! Are you one of them? *Everywhere that is the case with you, everywhere you can't even say multimillionaire or can't even imagine being a part of that league, times a godzillion, will you destroy and uncreate it all now, please? Right and Wrong, Good and Bad, POD and POC, All 9, Shorts, Boys, and Beyonds.*

AN OPPORTUNITY IS NOT A POSSIBILITY

The two aspects have distinctively different energies. Let me explain this aspect with an example. Another school episode. In one of my classes, a lady shared her story about how she had failed to recognize the difference between the two.

Keen to start a school, this lady was looking for anyone who was ready to strike a business deal with her. She grabbed the first opportunity that knocked at her door. Immediately she assumed (and concluded) that this was the precise prospect for her. There were three parties: backers (the financial people), clients (the kids), and personnel. Desperate to close the deal, she was ready to take any step. Ironically, though, whenever she would come close to finalizing the deal, something would pop up. This ordeal lasted for twenty months. Eventually, the deal fell apart.

She discovered later that the backers were trying to close the same deal with two different businessmen at the same time. All along, she kept feeling heavy energetically. In spite of all her efforts, nothing seemed to work out. Yet, against all odds, she wanted this reality to manifest for herself.

How do we understand the difference between a *Possibility* and an *Opportunity*? An *Opportunity* can sometimes have a hollow feeling attached to it, like a trapdoor. This may even feel like vertigo, as if we are about to fall into a void. Other times, an *Opportunity* can make us feel like we have hit a brick wall or that we have reached a dead-end street.

The hollow or vertigo feeling usually shows up when there is something wonky going on, or when we are missing some information, while the brick wall is how we feel when we come to a roadblock. Either way, sooner or later we reach the same result: nowhere to go. It is as though initially it looked good and smelled good, but it was only a distraction. Whether it is the feeling of vertigo or that of a brick wall, they are both indicative of an *Opportunity*. One drags us into a scam where we feel all whooshed up; the other one looks good, but it is a facade. There is nothing behind that wall.

The energy of a *Possibility* is quite different. It is full of excitement and joy and fun, and there are always more questions and more choices that come from it. It is like being on a never-ending highway of possibilities. While the vertigo we feel when confronted with an *Opportunity* may seem like the bottom has fallen out, a plethora of *Possibilities* is like the roof has been raised and "the sky's the limit."

Here are a few questions we can ask to get a clearer picture:

> Is this an opportunity or a possibility?
> If I choose this, will it add to my life today and bring me more money right away, and in the future?
> Is this an investment or expense here? (time, money, energy)
> What is the future I am not preparing for?
> Where is the money I am not seeing?
> Can I have the money now, please?

The following questions are some of my personal favorites:

> What question can I ask here that will give me some different choices and present some different possibilities?
> What am I not willing to look at here?
> How can I look at this from a different perspective?

Here are the three wonderful gifts these questions offer:

> 1. Awareness of the energy of a different choice
> 2. Awareness of the energy of when someone is stalling or lying
> 3. Awareness of the energy of when it is not the right moment: too late, too early, or not the best choice at the present time

If we are willing to recognize these three energies, it gives us ample clarity and choice about the ongoing predicament, or what seemed like an expansive possibility in the beginning but turned out to be a limited opportunity with time.

When there is some kind of a deal being struck, or somebody is talking to us about a possibility to explore— say, a house, trip, car, business deal—these are some good questions to ask:

> Am I missing some information here?

How many people are involved in this deal?

Do I need to talk to anybody else about this?

How many hurdles / other people do I have to go through before I get the "go ahead" here?

For instance, if it is a house we are interested in buying:

How long has this house been on the market?

Has it changed hands many times?

Is it debt free?

Is there any family mess or other entanglements going on here that will hinder my purchase?

If someone offers us a partnership, a new endeavor, or business proposal:

Who or what is the valuable product here?

Is this an opportunity or a possibility, now and in the future?

What will my life and money situation be like in five years if I sign this deal?

What will my life and money situation be like in five years if I choose to do something else instead?

What will the planet be like in fifty years if I opt for this?

Is it in sync with where I desire to go?

Will it be a contribution?

Regarding the last question—Will it be a contribution?—if we do not specify anything (for example, "Will it be a contribution to me, my life, or my goal?"), the universe takes ALL things into consideration. The energetic response we get, once we are willing to receive information from the universe to help us decide, is much more accurate and all encompassing than any calculations or solutions we can arrive at, using our cognitive skills.

When we ask what it will create in five years, we skip any reasoning abilities that may get in the way of the energetic awareness. Gary Douglas rightly says that five years is usually a longer period of time for even the most-rational thinkers to figure out every single pro and con. What we get is the sensation of the energy that this choice will create in our lives. Next, we can ask if the sensation that we felt, when we asked the question, is an energy we would like to have more of in our lives. If it is a sensation of expansion and lightness, then it is probably something that will create more ease for us and get us closer to the life we desire (even though we have not yet figured out how to obtain it).

PROBLEM-SOLVING IS NOT A SOLUTION

When we are problem oriented or great problem solvers, we tend to concentrate more on identifying the problem. If there is not one, we often conjure one up, without even realizing it. It is almost as if we are missing that problem vibration in our lives.

Everywhere that you are so good at solving problems you must create them so you don't lose your job, times a godzillion, will you destroy and uncreate it all now, please? Right and Wrong, Good and Bad, POD and POC, All 9, Shorts, Boys, and Beyonds.

Likewise, when we are trying to avoid challenging situations, we often first invoke them, so we can get crystal clear about what we do not want. Then we start trying to change that situation and change the energy of that. What if we could simply choose something that is not challenging, not a problem at all, but a possibility?

We are usually pretty good at picking up on challenging problematic energies, but most of the time we do not follow our own instincts. We let the mind trick us into believing that we are indulging in negative thinking or judgments. Money can have all the energies around it—challenging, problematic, heavy, judgment ridden. Sometimes, a few questions might seem repetitive, but the energy of each question with a slight tweak is always different, and you get it when you get it. The simplest way to find out the truth is to ask some questions, to pick whichever one works best for you in that moment. So, keep asking even if it seems like it is the same question. The following are examples:

Is this situation flowing? Is it stuck?

Is there a hidden trapdoor here, a brick wall or a challenge that is not apparent?

What is this strange vibe I am getting here? Is it me, something else, or someone else?

Would it be easier and more joyful if I were to put my energy somewhere else? Would it bring me more money?

Is this an investment (time, energy, money) now or in the future, or is it an expense?

Is it worth my time, energy, and money?

Would putting my energy somewhere else create more money with more ease?

If we get frustrated about a situation, an ideal way to understand what is going on is to ask these questions:

What is this energy of frustration?

Is there something wrong here?
Is there a lie here somewhere?
Is there something I am not looking at?

These questions usually calm us down long enough to see some clarity in the situation. It creates enough distance between us and the situation.

We can ask more questions for better clarity.

How many times have my fixed points of view been instrumental in germinating a problem when there is not one?

How much am I willing to be aware of, so I do not find myself in a crisis situation like this in the future? All that hinders me from marching toward growth, times a godzillion, I now destroy and uncreate it all. Right and Wrong, Good and Bad, POD and POC, All 9, Shorts, Boys, and Beyonds.

Another powerful tool, ideal for such situations, is to make it infinite. Basically, keep expanding the denseness of the situation, and gradually it will no longer feel like a lead bomb.

Imagine that you have put a balloon at the center of the problem. Begin inflating that balloon. Bigger and bigger. As the balloon expands, either the problem gets more intense and more real, or it disintegrates and becomes more molecular. Inflate the balloon more. Make it as big as the universe. Now, look at the situation again. Is it still dense and intense or is it lighter now?

This is a great way to observe what part of the situation is a lie. Now, do the same thing with a situation that is going well for you, that brings you joy. Put a balloon at the center of the situation and inflate it. Blow it bigger than the universe. How does that situation feel now? Is it still joyful? Acknowledge the part that is true. The joy. Problems are usually a lie, and when you make them infinite, bigger than the universe, they disappear or lose their intensity. When you take something that is joyful and make it infinite, it usually brings you an even-deeper sense of joy.

In case of ambiguity, to set the ball rolling, explore more questions:

Does the ball want to roll?
Does the ball want to bounce or do something else?
Is this ball for me or for someone else?
What else is required here?
What else can I be or do here that I have never even imagined?
Okay, since the situation is not resolving the way I had thought it would, what else is possible?

IT IS TIME TO CHILL

If we keep feeling heavy each time we ask questions about a particular situation, it may mean we are being too rigid about how or when we want to receive the answers. For instance, "This is not what I was expecting." Or "Sorry, Universe; I'm too busy on Sundays, so let's stall the 'answer' for another day." Or "No, not on Thursday nights either. I have my favorite games to watch."

The universe always presents us with the best solution in any circumstance. It has no point of view about anything. That is precisely the reason why it has abundant information on any topic. When we have too many points of view and we get too finicky about what the answer should be, or what the answer should look like (in this case, money), or when the appropriate time is to receive it, we reject what could potentially be our best option. So, even if it shows up, we are unable to see or recognize it since we have narrowed our vision by solidifying possibilities into fixed points of view. Oh, yeah, and as my friend Dain Heer says, "It NEVER shows up the way we think it is supposed to."

JUDGE 'EM NOT

Judgments—positive or negative—are fixed points of view that block contributive energies from reaching us. We can't accept compliments from people we judge. Whenever we have some resistance toward something or someone, it is an area we are unwilling to receive from. For example, we cannot obtain money easily from people who annoy us. Our fixed, narrow points of view do not allow us to see what is beyond our judgments.

Then, there are categories of topics wherein our moral verdicts or ethical stance (often judgments) justify our unwillingness to receive anything from certain people, since we have already decided it is the wrong thing to do. For example, we would prefer not to charge people who are dying of cancer. Or we wouldn't want to take money from a convicted thief or a person of ill repute. It is our judgments (of any kind) that stop us from receiving abundance from all of the universe. And how do we build these judgments? We acquire them by buying other people's realities.

I grew up in a family where my mom and dad were diametrically opposite to each other with regard to judgments. While Mom was least opinionated about almost everything in life, Dad had a say about everything and everyone. Later in life, it dawned on me that I was more like mom. I was comfortable about many things around me. Not much rattled me.

For example, in my late teens, I was employed by a lady therapist who was a specialist in counseling gays, transsexuals, and transvestites. It was the first time I had seen this world at such close quarters. Yet, nothing scandalized me. Michelle, the name of the therapist, had gotten her gender changed.

Earlier named Michael, he had fathered two children. Now, she was living with another woman. In spite of hailing from conventional Boston, I found this kind of life interesting. People's sexual preferences or orientations never mattered to me.

Once, during Christmas, when I had accompanied Michelle to a party with people of different sexual orientations, it was fascinating to see people who were this honest and open about who they really were. I had only admiration for them. In general, since subconsciously my barriers were mostly down, I had built my own all-inclusive universe.

What could you receive from anyone and everyone if you had no point of view about who they were, who they loved, or what they chose as their lifestyle?

BEING NONJUDGMENTAL ABOUT MANIPULATING OTHERS

I had always considered *Manipulation* a form of psychological torture or abuse. Even if I had never articulated it quite that way, I realized that I had that point of view one day when someone accused me of being a good *Manipulator*. I cringed. The founder of Access Consciousness, Gary Douglas, gave me a different perspective on *Manipulation*. He asked, "Do you use the skills of *Manipulation* to invite people to do things they haven't yet decided to do? To encourage them to choose something greater for their life?" That matched much more the energy of what I do: use the skills of *Manipulation* to help people attract more in their lives. A space where people recognize their potential and get aware of what more they can create and receive. After this awareness, I started having fun with *Manipulation* and made it so obvious that people would laugh and more readily choose something greater. I also became more willing to receive *Manipulation* myself, to be *Manipulated* into choosing more in my own life.

For example, when I was supervising all the live and written translations of Access Consciousness, since work had grown exponentially, Gary asked me to expand the team. Observing my apprehension to do so, he asked, "What if you could step up from this role and run an international business, not just a piece of one?" Initially, I was resistant to this. *Would I no longer have my job as supervisor?* I wondered in dismay. After I calmed down, I asked questions and started recognizing some different possibilities of working with Access tools that involved more growth for me. It was then that I realized how Gary had "manipulated" me into choosing something greater than I had ever considered possible. This *Manipulation* inspired me to create my own company, and today I have an international business, and I invite others to create more in their lives and businesses. How does it get any better than that?

Initially, I had resisted manipulation. Now, I see that it can also be an invitation that you can either accept or decline. What if it was just an interesting point of view? Instead of resisting it, what if we could ask this: Is this going to create more for me?

Everywhere that I allow my judgment to supersede my awareness, times a godzillion, I now destroy and uncreate it all. Right and Wrong, Good and Bad, POD and POC, All 9, Shorts, Boys, and Beyonds.

I remember advising a mother to manipulate her kids. Her children were glued to their mobile phones almost all the time. Even during dinner. She had tried quite a few tactics to stop this practice, but she had failed. I found out they loved sweets. I asked the mother to manipulate the kids into leaving their gadgets for some time if they wanted to relish eating sweets. She had the judgment that being glued to any gadget for this long was bad for their health, but she wanted them to recognize this fact on their own. However, when I suggested that she give this tactic a try, she was willing to do it. The deal was this: to eat the sweets, they would have to enter a tech-free room. The children chose to enjoy having sweets over playing games on their phones. Not just that, while having their favorite sweets, the family got to enjoy some good-quality time together as well.

Here are a few questions we can ask in moments of despair, or even otherwise:

If I were not choosing doom and gloom, what would my awareness be?
What is right about this that I'm not getting?
What different choices can I make today so my reality changes?
What choice am I unwilling to make that, if I were willing to, it would change this condition?
What do I love about creating crises?

UNDERSTANDING JUDGMENTS BETTER

When we run into a judgment, we can ask these questions:

What am I refusing to be that, if were willing to be it, would set me free? (This one is a gift from Dr. Dain Heer, cocreator of Access Consciousness and author of Being You, Changing the World.)
How can I use this to my advantage?
What am I not willing to be aware of that, if I were willing, my reality would alter significantly?
What else is there to notice and be aware of that my judgment and conclusion thus far have not allowed me to see?
What if I used all the swirling controversies in the world and all the

judgments about them to make money?

People believe they have a right to judge. They have a fixed point of view about almost everything. What if we could use their judgments to our benefit?

When I was working for the Mediterranean Film Festival in Italy, I was asked to be the contact person for a French technical professional. I had accompanied him all day and had taken care of everything he had required. At the end of the hectic day, when we both were sitting and sipping some wine, he said to me, "So, you're American! I've never really liked them much. They think they are the center of the world." I could have reacted, defended . . . done all those usual things we do when someone throws a barb at us. Instead, I calmly responded, "You know, you are absolutely right. Not like the French, who think they are the center of the universe." He laughed and laughed and laughed. Then, he lifted his glass and said, "Cheers, we understand each other very well." From that moment on, we had a wonderful time working together. Later, he gave me a great recommendation too. This is a classic example of how we can use people's judgments to our benefit.

Apart from the abovementioned aspect, learning the delicate skill of manipulation can also help us increase income, for ourselves and for everyone else. I am talking about utilizing people's judgments to create something greater. If we get caught up in our fixed points of view and start resisting and reacting to people's judgments or behavior, then we go into judgment ourselves and eliminate possibilities. If, instead, we are willing to have no point of view, we can easily turn a judgment into a possibility that increases the ease, the joy, and the flow of money in our lives.

MAKING MONEY FROM JUDGMENTS

As human beings we have an innate tendency to react to a judgment—positive or negative. Either we agree and align with a positive judgment, or we defend and resist a negative one. This stops the energy flow. When we defend against someone's judgment—their truth—we try to prove it is not true. We are so busy defending that we miss out on the innumerable choices we have in front of us. When we align and agree, we buy their truth and stop asking questions and exploring or receiving other possibilities. If we get busy reacting to a judgment, how will we create something beyond that? How will we be or find something that can be a contribution?

I remember Gary Douglas saying, "For every judgment you are willing to receive, that you are not resisting, good or bad, you make 5,000 dollars more per year!" I thought to myself, here is an interesting way to make more money.

"She's a snob!"—"Thank you!"
"He's a jerk!"—"Thank you so much!"

"You're always so sassy."—"*Thank you!*"
"It's dirty money." (No judgment)

A lot of times we refuse the energy of money because most of the money that circulates in the world is generated by things that we have a judgment about. For example, arms dealings, drugs, human trafficking, extinct animals, etc. Many times we get the energy of it. It may be difficult for us not to react to that money when we come in contact with it, but what if we are willing to be the agent of change? Being the transformational energy that we are, no matter what energy is attached to money, what if we could change its energy and use it to create more consciousness in the world instead of less?

LOSING MONEY FROM JUDGMENTS

For every judgment we are unwilling to receive, we have a deficit of 10,000 dollars. Oops! Why is that? A judgment is a block of dense energy that someone is stuck in. When they throw that block at us, and we resist it, eventually we too get trapped in their heavy energy block. We stop creating more in our lives because we make that judgment more valuable than us.

Do others' judgments change or better us? No. They are simply their points of view. They are not real. We make them real and solid by accepting or resisting them.

Think about it—don't we feel bad when someone judges us negatively? That is sucking out our energy, isn't it? When we accept a compliment (which is often also a judgment), we are imprisoned in that particular point of view. In reality, we are always more than just that one single attribute, aren't we?

All the judgments I am not willing to receive, because I have a point of view about them, that is limiting my life, living, bank account, times a godzillion, I now destroy and uncreate it all. Right and Wrong, Good and Bad, POD and POC, All 9, Shorts, Boys, and Beyonds.

IN ALLOWANCE OF . . .

Allowance is—everything is just an interesting point of view. It is not bad; it is not good; it is just an interesting point of view.

> They are bad people because they make money off other people. (Interesting point of view)
> They are not good clients because they are always trying to get a discount. (Interesting point of view)
> They are losers because they never pay their bills on time. (Interesting point of view)

If we did not have a point of view about how other people make money, spend money, or pay their bills, we would be able to receive money from all people, always. Wouldn't we?

BEGIN WITH BASICS

At times, we are in a rush to prove to the world (or even to ourselves) that we have to "do" something. We have to be in the action mode to create more. In that hurry, we often get into doing things that are not truly a contribution to us.

How many times have we dived head-on into endeavors without being clear about some basic truths? Here are a few helpful questions to get some transparency:

Is this the best move for me at this moment?
Is now the time?
Is this even relevant in my life at this moment?

HANG ON . . . LISTEN TO THE *SILENCE*

When we ask questions to the universe, we don't have to jump to look for an answer immediately. Let our awareness be our guidance system. Hang on for a moment. For example, say, we ask, "Truth, what will my life be like in five years if I choose to do this project/venture/trip?" We have to wait until we get the feeling in our body or the sensation in our universe that will give us the information about the question we asked.

"Truth, what will my life be like in five years if instead I choose to do a different project/venture/trip?" We have to wait until we get the energy with the second hypothesis.

Now we can compare the two energies. Check which option makes us feel lighter. If we feel no difference, it is all right. There is nothing to worry about. Try again after ten minutes. Ask the same two questions about the same project. Keep at it. It took me quite awhile to recognize these kinds of subtle energies. With consistent efforts, I am now able to perceive it clearly. Life is much simpler now. Most times, I ask one of the simplest, yet potent, questions of Access Consciousness: *How does it get any better than that?*

SAVE 10%. BECOME A MILLIONAIRE.

I started earning at age twelve. My grandmother paid me to polish her silverware. She also gave me money when I helped her set up tables for her bridge (playing cards) tournaments. At thirteen, I did some odd jobs. At fourteen, I sold ice cream on an ice-cream truck. Throughout my teen years, I did many after-school and summer jobs. In college, I took up three jobs.

Ever since I started making money, Dad taught me the concept of saving. He educated me on the benefits of putting away 10% of every earning ever made. If only I had listened to him diligently, I would probably be a millionaire today. I got serious about this practice only in my adult life.

Access Consciousness teaches the same philosophy. The practice of putting aside 10% of what you earn radically changes your perspective about wealth. Money accruing on a regular basis gives a feeling of abundance. It is not a month-to-month salary scenario. Once putting aside 10% becomes a habit, we actually experience the sensation of having money. "You see it, you believe it"—this thought process of being present with abundance at all times in our lives attracts more wealth. Once we have amassed a decent sum, we can choose to invest it in a secure venture that will get us more money, or do something that will ensure that the money will not diminish. Money multiplies and fetches more money.

What if we followed this practice meticulously? We would become millionaires. What if we became multimillionaires?

There are tons of ways to make money, invite money, and enjoy money. If we are out of judgment, not problem oriented, looking for possibilities and not just following opportunities; if we are more interested in lightness and joy than doom and gloom, and drama and trauma, money will gladly find us.

Ask questions. Abundantly. This method will keep giving us clarity about any and every situation. Once we have gotten the hang of "asking questions and getting their energetic responses," we will automatically know how to go with the flow. Our intuition will give us strong signals about what to do next. Most importantly, we have to start saving 10% of WHATEVER amount we receive. Believe me, this practice will help immensely.

In Access Consciousness, the belief about *Money* is that money follows joy. We have to ask ourselves: *Are we willing to get into the flow of abundance and ride the wave of joy and money? Everything that doesn't alow that times a godzillion, we now destroy and uncreate it all. Right and Wrong, Good and Bad, POD and POC, All 9, Shorts, Boys, and Beyonds.*

CHAPTER 5

THE CAREER CODE: STYLE YOUR FUTURE

"I'm really sorry; I cannot take up your offer. Not sure of what I want to do next, but I'm confident that it's time to change paths," I told a senior associate. He had advocated for me for a management position in one of the most exclusive hotels in New York City. I had been in this industry in various positions for almost a decade. In an unexpected incident, I had lost my job. Taking up this magnificent offer would have been the apt step to take. Handsome salary. Fabulous perks. A job when I did not have one. What more could I have asked for?

Plenty more.

Standing at the crossroads of what could conventionally be described as a midlife crisis, I picked freedom of choice. I was willing to be uncomfortable long enough to see what I would truly like to create next. I asked myself, "What would it take for me to explore new horizons and set the bar higher without any inhibitions, apprehensions, and fears?" "What would I like to do if I could choose to do and be anything?" is a question that was reigning my subconscious mind. Funnily enough, I was being these tools before even hearing about Access.

Sometimes it is important to take a pause, bid time, so you seize that perfect moment for your true desires to bear fruit. One of my god-daughters wrote this on a social media platform recently: "Looks like I'm wasting time." Was she? I called to check on her.

Waiting need not necessarily symbolize procrastination. How can you tell the difference? Ask these questions:

Truth, am I procrastinating?

Truth, am I missing some information here?

Truth, is this the right time to do that?

[Think of a career and ask,] *Truth, is this the right vocation for me to choose?*

Truth, is some other profession better for me?

Truth, is something else going to show up that is going to create more?

Truth, is there something that I may be aware of but haven't brought into focus?

When you are unsure of what move to make next, ask the following:

What is my point of view here?

Is this even my point of view?

What if I could pick any profession I like?

What would that feel like?

What would I pick?

Either these questions will help you get a clearer picture or you will feel lost in a void. If you feel ambiguous about the next move, observe: Does the question lead to a response or trigger an awareness to ask another question? After every question you ask, PAUSE. Wait for the energy of that question to stir some things up, and ask your next question on the basis of that energy that comes up.

Have you ever noticed how tranquil waters in a pond enable us to admire the fish that swim deep within? Similarly, these "pauses" offer us clarity, so we can pick that which would be the greatest contribution to us in the future. Though to many, such sudden changes may seem like failures, that is an enormous misidentification of the situation. These are usually moments when choosing the best option and the greatest change are possible.

CHANGE IS GOOD

The willingness to change anything that is not working is the source of true happiness and success. It does not mean you have to change anything immediately. You need not have to do anything at all, either. You just have to be willing to acknowledge the energy and the potential for the transformation. It is your willingness that will give you the power and motivation to choose what is going to create more.

Have you noticed how energetically light and exciting it feels when you have an unlimited range of career paths to choose from? If you are unwilling to change, you get to pick only from your limited reality. *Every time and everywhere that you limit your thinking due to fear of change, times a godzillion, will you destroy and uncreate it all now, please? Right and Wrong, Good and Bad, POD and POC, All 9, Shorts, Boys, and Beyonds.*

Sometimes you may think you desire change, but in reality, you prefer to conform. If you get fixated with the outcome of what change will bring about, if you believe the result has to appear in a particular manner, know that you are living a facade. Change with a preordained conclusion is a falsity. Unless you allow the willingness to change to be the core navigator of your journey, without having a fixed point of view of what the end should look like, be prepared to stay where you are.

When you ask the universe (via questions) to help you manifest a new reality—say, more money or ease in business, the responses you receive are for your highest good. They are a culmination of the collective consciousness that is available throughout the universe. It is the best the universe has to offer at this time, on the basis of what you are able and willing to receive. Can you fathom the magnitude of "search" here? But if you are unwilling to look at all options, you have already limited your possibilities. For all you know, that possibility might never need to be exercised, but any awareness or information associated with it will not be available to you either. Who knows, some trickling information about career change that you truly desire to take might be hidden in an idea that you refuse to even consider. If you exclude anything, you may never receive the rainbow waiting for you behind a seemingly black cloud.

Everywhere that you limit your options before you have even considered all of them, times a godzillion, will you destroy and uncreate it all now, please? Right and Wrong, Good and Bad, POD and POC, All 9, Shorts, Boys, and Beyonds.

CHOOSING WHAT IS VITAL FOR YOU

"How do I know what's right for me? What career do I choose?" These are questions that people commonly ask me. My reply to them is uncomplicated—look for what matters most to you. What is vital to you? What is it that without which you feel incomplete? For example, I am a big talker, the environment is really important to me, and I really don't like pushy people. Whenever I have chosen a career, I have kept these factors in mind.

Keep asking questions. Don't get into the "How will they manifest?" part of your desires. Whether you want to be part of the corporate world or you are keen to be an entrepreneur, the rules are the same for the career game. First, know what works for you. Second, choose what works for you. Third, change what does not work for you.

Is there a project that you like? What are the elements needed to bring a project to life? You need a *Creator*—someone who is able to create a new project; a *Connector*—someone who is able to talk to people, get people interested in the business; and a *Mover*—who is actually going to get work done at the ground level. Where do you find yourself? What are you good at (even if you have been chastised for being that)? We have all three of these aspects within us, but there is a predominant character in us that outshines the other parts.

These are some more questions that you can ask yourself:

What is my skill set?
What is my unique brand of magic?
How do I utilize that stuff in any project: creator-connector-mover?
How do I propose myself in a career that speaks to what is vital to me?
What have I been accused of being too much of or not enough of? (For example, in your childhood if you were always reprimanded for being talkative, know that you are a good talker. Keep in mind that is one of your core skills.)

READY TO SOAR

For the longest time, Gary would say, "You have to be willing to step over people's heads if you want to get ahead in life." Each time I thought of this strategy, I would be hit with a heavy feeling. I kept telling myself I was not willing to step on anyone's head. Even if I were drowning, and stepping on a floating dead body was my only chance to survival, I would still not be able to do that. And that was the point of Gary's statement. I got that years later. And I do mean years.

Anywhere you are not willing to do something, you will be at the behest of people who are willing to do it.

And again, just because you are willing to do it does not mean you will ever have to. It just touches on that area of your life where you are already functioning from conclusion; where you are not even willing to ask a question, because you have already decided what you will never do. When you have decided what you will never do, you can't even play with the energy around that topic. You can't play or talk or hear anyone who is willing to do that which you are not willing to do. You enter into limiting judgments that limit you, your life, your career, and your pursuit of happiness. There was a point in time when I was not willing to do many things. Over the years, I have changed a bit.

What is it that you are unwilling to do, even if it is creating more for yourself and others, because you have decided that this is a bad thing to do? Such as a divorce. A change of job. Or a change of profession even. End a friendship. Say no to someone. *Everywhere that you stop contributing to your growth because of your preconceived notions and fixed judgments, times a godzillion, will you destroy and uncreate it all now, please? Right and Wrong, Good and Bad, POD and POC, All 9, Shorts, Boys, and Beyonds.*

The willingness to be and do and change anything and everything gives you a different approach to life. When you step into the world from a space of awareness, people do not take advantage of you. For instance, when I was reelected for a second term as president of a voluntary organization, initially it went well. Later, though, I decided to quit. In spite of me sharing my thoughts with the concerned professionals, they were no longer responding to me. Maybe they thought I would never ever leave that position, so they took my concerns and suggestions lightly. Since I had waited months without any response, I realized that a different energy was needed, and that my staying on was not creating more for me or the organization. I knew that if I had warned them that I was thinking about resigning, they would have tried to convince me otherwise, again making promises that they had no intention of following through with. So instead, I called for an emergency board meeting and advised them of my decision to quit, seconds before hitting the send button on my farewell email to the entire membership.

Dare to be yourself. Always.

A NEW START

Starting a new business is a journey that is always unique to every entrepreneur. Most people shudder at the thought of starting something on their own. They presume that doing business may not be fun, or that it may not make a lot of money. A few years ago, after having worked and helped many others grow their ventures, I decided it was time I invested my time and energy to create magic for me.

I was aware I had a plethora of rich experiences. They were not just varied in nature; they were unique too. This is one aspect that most people do not realize and acknowledge. Always know that you are unique; hence your approach to everything in life is different from other people. Cash in on that factor. This realization is the key to success.

Speaking about me, one of the aspects that constitute my unique brand of magic is the fact that I have worked, lived, and loved in different countries, in different languages, and in different professions. This sensibility makes me extremely marketable.

What is your niche?
What are your USPs (unique selling points)?

Being aware of the general rule of thumb in business—niche, target customer, and demographic—I knew that had I wanted to succeed, I would have to narrow down my target career that would cater to one niche, one type of customer, and one geographical area. But how was I to do that? And why would I do that? The very thought of starting my business by using this model made me feel smaller, contracted, limited. If I would feel such dense energies while doing my business, then I would rather find a conventional job and make lots of money.

To get more clarity on the subject, I started asking more questions. I started interacting with the energy of all those queries I bombarded at the universe—*what energy, space, consciousness, and choice can I be that will allow me to create a business and a life not only in this reality, but one that will go beyond this reality?*

These are the kinds of questions I asked and continue to ask daily about my life and my business. The responses I receive always have to do with being everything I am, without excluding anything.

I conduct classes in different countries and online, in different languages, and talk on a variety of topics: business, money, relationship, body, race, energy, family, empowerment, women, the Earth, and me. I travel around the globe. I have friends in different parts of the world. I have an amazing personal life. How does it get any better than that? When people ask me what I do, I proudly share, "I change people's lives by getting them present to new ways of thinking and being." This alone helps people make better choices in their own life. I create magic in my life, and the mere fact that people observe me doing and being that allows them to recogne what is best for them, and they too begin creating magic in their lives.

Sometimes, many people show up at my conferences, and sometimes, very few, but the number game does not dissuade me anymore. As long as I follow my true self, I am a success. My business is a success. My life is congruent with the invitation and the possibility I want to be and receive in the world.

If you trust your intuition and are willing to ask questions that truly open up more possibilities from which you can choose, you are already on the path of success. Then you can invite and receive contributions from the entire world, and the universe will conspire to support you.

CHAPTER 6
PURPOSE OF LIFE OR LIVING PURPOSEFULLY?

Let's consider two possibilities:

Option 1: Say that early on in life, you decided, like your parents, you would like to be an engineer too. You never allowed yourself to think of any other career option. Though you detested studying those subjects, you kept at it. As a young adult, you are now an engineer. But that is all of who you are. You do not have a social life that excites you. You do not have any close friends. You have no experience of how the world works. Now that you have gotten thrown into the deep end of life, you are drowning.

Option 2: As a kid, like most others, your goals kept changing in each grade. Eventually, you started paying keen attention to the vocations that excited you. You went with the flow and kept exploring new possibilities, since they kept presenting themselves to you. Some moves worked in your favor, while some took you back a few notches (or so it seemed). No matter what your experiences were, you enjoyed the journey through and through. After all, all those experiences have made you who you are today.

Of these two options, which one is closest to you?

There is absolutely nothing wrong in setting a fixed purpose in life and working toward achieving it, as long as there is joy in doing what you are doing. But if you are dealing more with *"Monday blues"* than *"Saturday night fever,"* it is time you rethink your strategy. Constantly living in judgment (how far or close am I from my goal) is more about surviving or merely existing rather than living and enjoying life.

Next, let's presume that you have achieved what you set out to accomplish.

Does that indicate that this is the end of your road? For the rest of your life, what will you look forward to doing and achieving? That is an enormously heavy energy to be engulfed in.

Living life purposefully implies that you are always enjoying what you are doing. It means you are living life to the maximum. When you are continuously in a space of creation, you are always growing, evolving, and generating more for yourself and others.

BANE OF WISHFUL THINKING

Instead of being open to change, if we stick to some prefabricated world of dreams, we manipulate our thoughts to fit in that concocted "reality." We force ourselves to believe that no matter what, they will manifest someday. We filter what we hear, clinging on to what we want to believe in (irrespective of the actual truth). Even if we are aware of hard facts about that aspect of life, we wish to believe that it will alter eventually. We choose to live in our bubble reality. For example, say someone is having an affair with a married person and chooses to believe that *that* reality will change someday. In spite of being categorically told that will never happen, this person is insistent on creating a "reality" that helps him or her escape from the actual truth.

If we are open to change, if we are willing to see another perspective, a lot more can open up and be available to us. For instance, if this person were to ask, "What if I could start afresh? Paint on a new slate?" Maybe something dynamically different could show up. A possibility that could transform their life and living in a manner they may have never imagined. All of these because the individual truly allowed the universe to engage in his or her life and was not vested in the outcome.

Gary Douglas once pointed out to me that I was good at asking a question about a situation and was open to receive a completely different point of view. He mentioned how my awareness helped me pick the best from a plethora of possibilities that question offered. People who like to remain stuck in their rut have accused me of playing *devil's advocate*. Little do they know that I take their judgment as a compliment.

What is limiting my imagination?
What is it that I am capable of that my imagination cannot grasp?
What am I capable of that I don't even know I am capable of?
What am I capable of that I know is possible, yet I have not dared to claim?
What am I capable of that I am pretending not to be capable of?
What am I capable of that, if I allow myself to be that, will expand my universe and give more meaning to my life?

How much do I know that I am refusing to know, because it does not make sense? If I were not trying so hard to make sense of it, would I get the clarity I have been seeking but just have not been willing to receive? Times a godzillion, I now destroy and uncreate it all. Right and Wrong, Good and Bad, POD and POC, All 9, Shorts, Boys, and Beyonds.

IT IS A RISKY MOVE

A dear friend was looking to hire someone to make phone calls for his business. He met a guy who did not fit the job profile at all, but he was willing to take a risk, so he hired that man anyway. The employee was bright and brilliant at other things, but making calls was not his forte. They worked together on numerous projects, until the two became partners. The employer is Gary Douglas, founder of Access Consciousness, and the young man is Dr. Dain Heer, its cocreator (when the two first met, Dain was a chiropractor). Today, together they run a booming business.

I have made my fair share of risky moves. Some paid off. Some did not, or so it seemed then. After all, today I am running an international business because of all the choices I kept making along the way—a revelation that struck me at my college reunion.

When I was asked to give a talk to the senior class at my alma mater, initially I wondered what I would emphasize on. My unconventional career path had been more a maze than a straight ladder. As I pondered deeper, I realized I was good at handling anything and everything, because I had never restricted myself from trying out a new and novel possibility. I never gave in, never gave up, never quit. I was open to explore any path. I was willing to do all it took to keep moving forward in life.

On my way back home, I thought to myself that in hindsight, I had come a long way. My original plan was to marry a good-looking, educated guy with a career (which I did—my first husband), have 2.5 children, and lead an upper-middle-class life in New York City. My kids would go to a good school. We would have an active social life, and we would go for vacations with family and friends . . . the usual stuff. I had not ever planned to live in Italy. Even when my ex-husband and I discussed about living in Europe, each time we did that, the possibility seemed to get further and further away. Something else always showed up. Yet, here I am—content with where all my choices have brought me.

IT IS ACTION TIME

It was not this idealistic when I moved here two decades back. We create our destinies—our victories, our pitfalls, our lives. I had worked in an array of industries in different capacities. All the experiences—interacting with people, traveling abroad, organizing events, etc.—had been quite enriching. The one aspect missing was spiritual fulfillment.

Shortly after I had put this thought out in the universe, I heard that Deepak Chopra, a spiritual guru, was coming to Rome. Back in my college days, I had read many books he authored. Those were the days when I used to go to different mind-body-spirit festivals, read inspirational books, visit channelers ... here in this European city, not much of all this was present.

I wanted to attend Deepak's conference, but I did not have the money to pay for the workshop. I did not want to borrow money from anyone either. I kept asking what else is possible. Eventually, to check things out, I called the event organizer to inquire if I could contribute in any capacity. After all, I knew four languages, and I had been in the hospitality sector at senior positions. I was sure there would be something I could do. I did contribute: I was at the event reception assisting participants. My language skills came in handy. Eventually, I got the class for half the price, an amount I could pay. How does it get any better than that?

MONEY & SPIRITUALISM—A HEALTHY OR DEADLY COMBO?

It is a standard belief (almost everywhere across the globe) that if we are in the field of social service (meaning, doing something that is a contribution to the society), we do not need to be financially remunerated. Receiving money for our contribution would be an insult to the service we are offering. It would somehow be untruthful. We would rather be a starving artist or live meagerly than get paid for our services. Have you ever met someone who feels like this, or is it the person you see in the mirror?

What have we made so vital about doing important work and being a contribution to others that doesn't allow us to receive gratitude and abundance as a thank-you from the universe? Everything that is, times a godzillion, let's destroy and uncreate it all now, please? Right and Wrong, Good and Bad, POD and POC, All 9, Shorts, Boys, and Beyonds.

Look beyond the superficiality of judgments. If we are doing work that contributes to the well-being of society, and are being paid handsomely for it, would not earning a handsome salary give us even more time for our work and make it even easier for us to continue contributing to society? Would not that help everyone in the process, including us?

Where have we bought the lie that by doing good deeds, God's work, we do not deserve to be compensated? Everything that is, times a godzillion, let's destroy and uncreate it all now, please? Right and Wrong, Good and Bad, POD and POC, All 9, Shorts, Boys, and Beyonds.

FEAR OF THE FUTURE

As a race, we believe in creating a better future. What is wrong with that, you may ask. If we trust that we have abundant wealth today and work toward generating more, we are playing it right. However, if we are operating from a place of skepticism, we are operating from a premise of fear. It subtly signifies that our future may not be secure, so let's lock in this money now (in the name of investment). There is no flow in a lockdown. No choice, no freedom.

What if we are willing to invest our money and keep asking questions about it? Everywhere that we are trying to secure our future instead of continually generating and creating it, times a godzillion, let's destroy and uncreate all now, please? Right and Wrong, Good and Bad, POD and POC, All 9, Shorts, Boys, and Beyonds.

Everywhere that we are buying a product or service or accepting a job on the basis of our hopes and dreams, projections, expectations, or judgments, or on the basis of the hopes and dreams of someone else, including those who are trying to sell us the goods, services, or the position, times a godzillion, let's destroy and uncreate all now, please? Right and Wrong, Good and Bad, POD and POC, All 9, Shorts, Boys, and Beyonds.

Every time and everywhere that we invest in someone or something, check out, and, after a while, forget to check back in periodically to make sure our point of view is still one of creation and not of scarcity, times a godzillion, let's destroy and uncreate it all now, please? Right and Wrong, Good and Bad, POD and POC, All 9, Shorts, Boys, and Beyonds.

Sometimes we are scared to look too closely at our situation (career, financial, talents, and abilities) for fear of jinxing them. We believe that if we continually keep checking in on our situation, acknowledging the successes and examining the challenges, we may jinx it or diminish it. What if we are afraid to admit to ourselves the riches that we have?

Everywhere that we have bought fear as our reality and are therefore unwilling to generate and create an even better reality, times a godzillion, let's destroy and uncreate it all now, please? Right and Wrong, Good and Bad, POD and POC, All 9, Shorts, Boys, and Beyonds.

The perfect way to handle any situation is to keep it alive in our awareness and periodically check in on the energy. Each time we do it, when there is a shift, we will know. Then, we can ask more questions and do the needful. Most importantly, it is best when we are not vested in the outcome. Movement, flexibility, and different possibilities cease to exist when we function from a rigid point of view—my way or the highway.

What if I am willing to change my moves at the drop of a hat?
What if everything is the opposite of what it appears to be, and nothing is the opposite of what it appears to be?

What if everywhere I have programmed and projected and expected and decided and concluded and judged about how the future will be, and how things are going to turn out, is not any longer true? Everything that doesn't allow me to have ease with any outcome, times a godzillion, I now destroy and uncreate it all. Right and Wrong, Good and Bad, POD and POC, All 9, Shorts, Boys, and Beyonds.

What limitation have I made more valuable than I am?
What point of view have I made so vital that I would rather perish than change it and choose something different?
What have I decided that I need that I actually don't need, which if I were willing to release that point of view of need, it would give me all of me?
Who have I decided I need that I actually don't, who if I were willing to let him or her go, it would give me all of me?

PURPOSE OF LIFE OR LIVING PURPOSEFULLY

My first career was in the hotel industry. Next stop was the entertainment industry—theater, music, film, and television. From 1996 to 2007, my association with organizing film festivals kept me busy. Later, I joined a new television film festival run by the State Department. In 2000, I produced an Italian film called *Sister Smile*. It was presented in a few film festivals, along with a series of short films and public-service announcements. One of them was presented by Kofi Annan at the United Nations. How does it get any better than that?

I even appeared as an actress in a couple of popular music videos. They were popular Italian and American singing groups. The Italian number was called *Athena Was Black*, and the American song was titled *Aquarius*, by my friend Karen Jones.

Life got even better when my friend Karen introduced me to Access Consciousness in February 2005. Ever since, I have been closely associated with this "way of life."

I have authored a book titled *7Steps to Flawless Communication*. It has already been translated into twenty languages! I am aware of the fact that there are many other possibilities that I can tap into, since the book has been very well received around the globe. I conduct business training and specific courses based on my book. I travel the world facilitating classes both on Access Consciousness and *7Steps to Flawless Communication*. During the Covid pandemic, I transformed my live business to an online business in just two months and started a new coaching program so that I could easily accompany people online during these times of change: 3 STEPS Journey Step In, Step Up, Step Out, a holistic approach to life and living. And what else is possible now?

Had I planned any of this? Not really. The only two constants while pursuing all these callings were, first, I had no reservations about doing any conventional job. I even waitressed during my college years. (I totally respect that profession, since it is a lot of hard work. And I did work very hard.) And second, I always was willing to enjoy the riches that each experience presented. There were ample times when I struggled, faltered, failed . . . but what kept me going was my following the energy of what was real and true for me, even if it meant taking the less traveled road. Would I have wanted it any other way? Nah. Nothing can beat the thrill of living life fully.

Like me, you have probably had a wealth of experiences. You have come a long way, baby. Been there, done that too. No matter how the journey has been, you can always choose a new point of view, change your step, and create a new reality for yourself. For me, life is about recognizing the beauty in every moment. Staying present with the changes and being willing to ebb and flow. If you don't like the music, change the tune.

Find the rhythm that works for you and enjoy dancing with the riches of your life.

Going forward, how would you like your life to be? All that stops you from creating the most fulfilling life for you, times a godzillion, will you destroy and uncreate it all now, please? Right and Wrong, Good and Bad, POD and POC, All 9, Shorts, Boys, and Beyonds.

May the Force be with you.

MORE ON KASS THOMAS

Hello,

Here is a list of the classes and workshops I conduct on a regular basis online and around the world.
Many of these classes are available online as well, so please check in with me to see what is new and what else is possible. You can either visit my website for more information or write to me at info@kassthomas.com. Hope to connect with you somewhere soon.

7steps to Flawless Communication
7steps Intro (2-hour introduction)
7steps Prelude (1-day class)
7steps Explosion (2-day workshop)
7steps to Abundance (2-day workshop)

Dancing with Riches
Dancing with Riches Intro (2-hour introduction)
Dancing with Riches Workshop (2-day workshop)

Access Consciousness Classes
Access Bars (1-day class)
Access the Foundation (4-day class)
Access Energetic Facelift Class (1-day class)
Access 3-Day Body Class (3-day class)
Access Your Communication Genius (1-day class)

3 STEPS Journey
Step In, Step Up, Step Out
(3-month, 6-month, and 1-year Programs)

For more information on any of the above, please write to info@kassthomas.com.

Or visit
www.kassthomas.com
www.7steps.us
www.accessconsciousness.com/kassthomas
www.3STEPS.us